# BLOOD, SWEAT & SPIKES

## RUNNING THE WETMORE WAY

a memoir by
**LYLE SMITH**

zolly house press

Published by Zolly House Press.
Longmont, CO 80503

Zolly House Press is an imprint of Nymblesmith.
zollyhouse.com

This book is a work of memory. All characters are based on the recollections of the author and all stories are as true as his memory will allow. Some names have been changed to protect the innocent and mostly innocent, but every story contained herein is told with great love, honor, and respect.

© 2024 by Lyle Smith.
Book & cover design by Zolly House Press.
Cover photograph by Lyle M. Smith Sr.
Inside photos courtesy of John Peterson, Sharon Siedliski, Holly Ahearn, Jennifer Rahn, Jim Nielsen, and Lyle Smith Sr.

Library of Congress Control Number: 2024924766
Identifiers: ISBN 979-8-9892659-9-2 (hardcover) | ISBN 979-8-9892659-8-5 (hardcover) | ISBN 979-8-9892659-7-8 (paperback) | ISBN 979-8-9892659-4-7 (paperback) | ISBN 979-8-9892659-6-1 (ebook)

All rights reserved. This book or parts thereof may not be reproduced in any form without permission.

Also by Lyle Smith
- Why Yellow Matters

To Mark. With profound thanks.
And for my dad.

"The greatest hazard in life is to risk nothing. The person who risks nothing, has nothing, does nothing, is nothing. That person may avoid suffering, pain, embarrassment, but that individual will not learn, grow, feel, love, or change. Only the person who takes risks is truly free."

- Chris Eubank,
WBO Super-Middleweight Champion

# Runners Set...

It's race day and I didn't know and I'm terrified. School lets out and the feeling is overwhelming my sixth-grade, 10-year-old self. Instead of trotting down to the field to warm up with the others, I turn tail and run home.

My heart beats hard. Jumping out of my chest. I feel like I may never catch my breath. My mind will not be distracted and the ground feels like it is falling away behind my heels. A vast chasm appears in my imagination as the earth cracks open a deep, dark hole behind me. Coming closer. Ready to swallow me whole even as I glance back to see what's chasing me and see nothing out of the ordinary. But I know it's there. My vision is focused to a pinhole. I see only one thing through my silent, overwhelming tears. Not forward. Just away. All I can do is keep running.

And no one and nothing can help me. I'm all on my own. All I can think is to get away. A mile down the road to safety. Quiet. My own space.

How did I get into this situation in the first place? I can't think of it. I'm just a kid. Why am I scared? I don't know. Fear of what? Embarrassment? Not being prepared? Losing? It's only a race across a bright green field on a sunny fall day. But it feels like a threat to my very existence. So I run. And I hide. And I hope none of the others will notice me missing.

But Mark notices. And he drives his white van down from the Polo Grounds to find me at home even though he has other important things going on a mile away. He cares about me more than I understood. He talks to me. Listens to me. Convinces me that I'm safe, and I'm ready, and it's time to go back and face the music I've been training for. I'm not sure what'll come of it all. But with that little bit of outside confidence, that feeling that he believes in me, I'm game to give it a go.

That's my coach. My teacher. My friend. It's what trust feels like. So I wipe my salty eyes dry and ride the mile back to the starting line. Where it all begins.

# Introduction

I got to know Peter Walsh after Coogan's closed. For good. Not the first time. Peter doesn't figure in the story directly, but hang with me and you'll see how he clicks in.

To explain Coogan's is to explain friendship. It can only be felt in that warm, deep, dropping into a favorite chair in front of the fire kind of a way.

In fact, Coogan's was a tavern at 4015 Broadway in Washington Heights sitting on the same long block of 169th Street as the old Armory where the world came to run at one time or another. Coogan's was a shelter during the more volatile moments in the neighborhood's history. It was a social, political hub. It was one of the few places in America that captured that essence of the Irish village pub experience. To those who'd been there dozens or hundreds of times, it was home. To those who walked through its doors for the first time, it was home. Uniquely welcoming.

Coogan's was also a track bar.

I'd been there when my sister, Emily, lived in the neighborhood. We ran Coogan's Run. I'd met Peter, but didn't know him. That came later.

Two beloved institutions were struck low on the same week in 2020. The Penn Relays was cancelled for the first time in its 126-year history and Coogan's closed its doors for good. Penn would come back. Coogan's would not.

Thanks to an introduction from my friend Meg Waldron, I was able to interview Dave Johnson that afternoon from his back garden outside of Philadelphia. Dave was the longtime meet director at Penn who had to make the call and like so many calls in those weeks, it was 100 percent the right thing to do, and 100 percent impossibly sad.

Dave put me in touch with Peter who enthusiastically agreed to talk to me on my Story Forge Podcast. One of those larger than life personalities you only cross paths with a few times in your life, Peter is the most important figure in American running you've never known. A track fan of the first order and a connector of the people. Peter Walsh has led the life of a warrior poet. A true Irish love who never let anyone go hungry.

Interviewing him was like trying to capture the wind. He told me so many things—so many stories, but for this purpose, he made a point of saying there's never been a "great running movie"—or book—and that's one of the things that has me sitting here with a sharpened pencil in my hand. I took it as a challenge.

This book is my own personal memory of something I think may be important to the people who lived it with me. Some who knew me well. Others who knew me as a very young kid. Some who didn't know me much at all. A thank you to the people who loved me and those I loved as much as the sport we all did. It is a thank you to the family I chose and earned along the way. These people who, if I'm honest, made as much of an impact as anyone on my time here on this planet.

It is part memoir, part remembered historical record, a love story and a cautionary tale. It is not an instructional manual despite it containing a record of more than a few of the workouts we did. There is no overarching training plan, so beware anyone who looks at this as some kind of recipe book. There is no revelation of the secret.

## WHY DID I WRITE THIS?

I've always been a writer. I started writing poetry after my mom introduced me to Robert Louis Stevenson's Child's Garden of Verses that my grandmother loved. That's undoubtedly where I began leaning toward nostalgia.

> "The rain is raining all around.
> It falls on field and tree.
> It rains on the umbrellas here.
> And on the ships at sea."

I'd never considered that it might rain at sea beyond the view of shore, but children only understand their own frame of reference—until they don't. Until they understand more. Adults, too, I think.

I wanted to be a cartoonist once. That was a kind of writer. But in a small school, the teachers only had limited holes for their pigeons and Jenny Chickering was "the artist." And Randy Grauerholz never accepted anyone else's fifth grade contributions, so I had to find something else.

Jenny was a terrific artist, by the way. Probably still is. No shakes on her. Her dad was a professional artist and someone I got to know later when I caddied for him up at the club. I just would have liked to have had a chance. I'm sure I'm not the only one.

## WHAT THIS BOOK IS.

The idea of this book has been banging around in my noggin for longer than I can begin to explain. I think longer than I understood, to be honest. I've always thought it a shame when facts and stories get forgotten or lost.

I know not everything is meant to be remembered, let alone remembered truthfully. And stories all evolve in the telling. Or carry the particular perspective of their narrators—and not all narrators are as reliable as the next.

But this is my version of this story. A story that's not all about me, but has been important to me. And who I was. Who I am. Who I've become.

The people I've known and watched and modeled myself after, whether they know it or not, are in this book. The people I met, but didn't know well, but were nevertheless important to me, are in this book. If you ever ran with me, you're probably in this book.

## WHAT THIS BOOK IS NOT.

Pure history. This is remembered history. So, by its nature, it is unreliable. Or not completely reliable. And told through the lens of my eyes and my flawed memory.

But more than anything, this is my way of trying to understand these things that made me. And my way of telling the world how much love fills the fuel tank of my heart and keeps my soul moving through the world powered by these things.

To have been a part of the Mine Mountain Road Department is to have a tribe that will never let you down. They understand your experience maybe better than anyone—maybe better than you do yourself.

This is my truth. And like Hemingway said of A Moveable Feast, "you may regard it as fiction, but there's always a chance it may throw some light on what has been written as fact."

LYLE SMITH

# The Memory

# 1

"The only sure thing about luck is that it will change."
- Bret Harte

I was 100 percent sure I'd be an Olympian when I got started. The gold medal was a question mark. I was pretty sure about it, but not 100 percent. The race and the travel and the Olympic village and the red, white, and blue warm ups—100 percent. I was about 11 years old.

I don't remember what we were training for, but it was the fall. It was raining like mad. And cold. Biblical rain. No letup. And I remember it was Homecoming at Bernards. Or Thanksgiving. Maybe it was the same. They set up lights on the track. Big, tall, towering scaffolds shining light down on the field so they could play football at night in the mud. So we couldn't use the track. The standards for the klieg lights were set on plywood platforms lane one through lane five. It made the place look important. Like something momentous was afoot there. We had to go somewhere else to work out. So John Peterson (JP) and I piled into Mark's little car to drive over to Mendham. That was the closest little town near our little town with a track we could use without anyone kicking us out. And the rain wouldn't stop. We had a 1500m time trial to do and we had to run through the puddles to prove it. We sat in the car watching the rain drive down. There were moments we couldn't even see the lane lines on the track.

You don't know what you don't know when you meet someone for the first time. And as much as you want to, you can't see what the future holds for other people. When I met him, Mark Wetmore was a young English teacher at Mt. Olive High School volunteer-coaching a youth running program in his hometown of Bernardsville. This was long before. Before the legend took root at the base of the Flatirons. Before the incredible success at the University of Colorado. Before the national championship teams and the Olympic and World Championship athletes. Before the World Cross Country qualifiers. Before *Running with the Buffaloes*. Before all the talk of training secrets and "The Wetmore Factor." Before even the Mine Mountain Road Department.

Mark Wetmore was my coach from the time I was in the fifth grade. He was just a kid himself at the time, really. A quiet, thoughtful, serious young man who was once the long-haired captain of the Bernards High School cross-country team who somehow managed to get us all to take his lead in the sport we all loved. You don't know what you don't know. Until you do.

The travel to train, of course, was nothing new to us. We'd often jump in a vehicle to get to a specific venue for a specific workout. What was unusual here was to go to another school's track where we waited as long as we could for the rain to let up even slightly so we could get out into our spikes to run.

I had some of the same nerves as race day. And at 11 or 12, we'd already had more experience with those than most adults.

The weather never did let up. Much. Not that time of year. Sometimes it socked in for days at a time. Late Fall weather in New Jersey. Gray. Wet. Raw. If you waited for good weather to go outdoors, you'd never go outdoors. So we went out into the weather to run hard anyway. Adjusting the expected splits and we did the work to get ready for the season to come.

I don't remember what the clock said. But I do remember the rain stinging my skin and feeling the cold splashing with every step. And that glorious satisfaction of slipping on my sweats when it was over. Tingly warmth flowing through me with every heartbeat and a lingering curiosity of how the football team would feel after losing their rivalry game in the mud that night. We were the same in some ways, I thought. But in others, nothing at all alike.

I would not be there. The football never really mattered to me.

# The Chocolate Man

# 2

"You cannot teach a man anything.
You can only help him discover it within himself."

- Galileo Galilei

It was the most frightened I'd ever been in my running life. Standing in the shade of the red brick stands past the starting line waiting for the clerk of the course to call the leadoff men to the line. I felt my heart beat slowly, but hard in the left side of my chest.

Thirty-eight thousand people to watch us race today was a lot to take in and a lot for a 14-year-old to shoulder—or not. I wasn't the only one. I could feel my spikes bottom out on the macadam just under the thin green track surface in the paddock. I noticed things in the paddock.

That's what they called it. The paddock where they shuffled us through. More than 15,000 athletes through their instructions. Sweats and numbers and safety pins. Tying and re-tying spikes to get just the right tightness so you don't lose your shoes or your circulation. Look down. Look up and you could lose your focus in the cheering faces. Or your lunch in the nerves of the moment. You're a performing clown at the carnival. Three days of the last weekend of April every year. That utterly unique blended aroma of mildew, liniment, and funnel cake still wafted out from under the stands into my nose assaulting my olfactory sense and lighting up my imagination.

My grandfather was Smitty. Ernest Lyle Smith. Born in Owego, New York, near Binghamton in 1920. I just learned that Rod Serling was a proud son of Binghamton and somehow, that made so much sense. Smitty was Lyle to his closest family, Ernest to the Army where he eventually worked his way up from Master Sergeant at the beginning of the war to Captain on Eisenhower's staff in London at the end. I should have asked him more about that when he was still around.

"Hey, Smitty!" It didn't register.

He ran the 220-yard low hurdles and played basketball in his day. I have his varsity "O" hanging on my wall with my dad's "PA" and my "B." He worked in a pool room where he once played against Ralph Greenleaf when the billiards ace was barnstorming across that part of the country so long ago.

But me, I was Lyle. Nobody called me...

"Hey! Smitty!"

I looked up, the first row about five and a half feet above the track surface perched atop that one-of-a-kind brick wall.

An enormous voice escaping the smiling white teeth of an equally enormous black man said, "Go get it!" as he reached out to shake my hand.

I didn't want to look up into the massive Franklin Field stands, afraid I might just freeze up completely and turn to stone. A man in a red windbreaker and blue baseball cap handed me a matching-colored baton. I remember noticing a small dent in the red side. Hey! I want a fresh one, I thought. I pictured a disappointed mile relay handoff from a previous year and promised the aluminum tube that I'd do my best to carry her cleanly around my three-lap assignment that afternoon. I peeked up to look at the battlements of the ancient-looking stadium and tried to relax. I took an enormous yaaaaaaawn and wondered why I always did that before a big race.

"Hey! Smitty!"

The voice I didn't know was calling to me from the front rows just above the exchange zone.

"Hey! Smitty!"

That's not me, I thought. That's grandpop.

I nodded and reached up to touch fingertips with this mountain of man who clearly knew more about everything than I did.

Who was this guy? I wondered, momentarily confused, gratefully broken away from my fear in the moment. He was clearly one of the historical touchstones of this place, mysterious and intimidating, but oddly emitting kindness. That much I could tell. And it made me feel warm in the terrifying moment.

My first Penn Relays experience was a year ago to the day. Friday at the Carnival. I cheered so hard for the Villanova men as they were soundly upset by the Arkansas Razorbacks for the first time. Then I hollered my heart out for my hometown Mounties in the High School Distance Medley, sure they would take the Championship of America going away. Stogryn on the opening 1200m leg to Sean Tutton on the 400m, our least natural distance, to Chris Blanchet on the 800m leg, to John Carlotti carrying anchor.

"Carlo!" we screamed, remembering doing the same last winter as he tried so desperately to escape the unnatural speed and determination of Mike Stahr on the yellow and orange boards of the Millrose Games inside Madison Square Garden.

Any sensible person would believe it was enough. A 4:06 leg with a several step lead just 200m to go. But Vance Watson drove through the roaring static of the crowd around that long, wide last turn and down the short finishing straightaway to dive at the tape in a dead heat victory: 10:00.9. The fastest ever for a high school team. Just an eyelash from going under 10:00 for the first time. Willingboro first. The most disappointing day.

And here I was, one year later, with a different, younger, less experienced foursome. Trying to prove we belonged here.

We knew we did, of course. We'd been thinking of little else since cross-country season ended.

And here I was, 4:50 in the afternoon on the last Friday of April wondering who this huge, man with an equally huge voice might be, cheering me on from the best seat in the house.

He must be someone important. But how does he know anything about me? This skinny sophomore from a tiny town 100 miles away?

They called us out of the shadow into the bright, warm, Philadelphia sunshine. We all, the leadoff men, striding backward up the straightaway to shake out our legs and shake out the dust of the paddock with long, strong strides, itching to hear the crack of the gun.

Then, they called us to the starting line for our final instructions.

**THE DISTANCE MEDLEY RELAY.**

Most track relays require four teammates to each run the same distance. The 4 x 400m relay — shorthanded "the mile relay" — is four runners each running 400m. The 4 x 100m, the other one most people are familiar with thanks to the Olympic Games. There's the 4 x 800m, the 4 x 200m, and in the early season relay meets, the longer and more exotic 4 x

1500m or 4 x 1600m (or 4 x mile) all based on the unexplained judgement of a meet head—meet director.

The Distance Medley, is a different animal asking each runner to race a different distance carrying a baton. The cool kids call it "the stick." The stick must be handed off from runner to runner within a specific exchange zone about 30m long, then carried across the finish line. If a team misses the zone, they're out. If a team drops the stick, they have to go back and get it and carry it across the line, otherwise they're disqualified.

The Penn Relays is the oldest and most famous annual track & field meet in the United States save the Olympics when it's here and US Olympic Trials. It has been run every year since 1895, the same year the modern Olympic Games was revived by Baron DeCoubertain. It's only missed one year in that entire time. Thanks to the COVID pandemic, the meet was cancelled in 2020 and reinvented as a smaller event later that year.

At Penn, today's Distance Medley (DM or DMR) is run with the 1200m leg (3 laps) as the lead-off runner, then a sprint single lapper (400m), then two laps (800m) for the gutsy half-miler, then the four sometimes fast, sometimes strategic laps of the anchorman miler. The one we trust to bring it all home.

Personally, I think it's the best event on the track. One that requires a complete team of runners—sprinters to distance runners—and all four have to be ready to run on that day, at that time. Together.

At Penn, the fast, invitation heats of these events are called The Championship of America.

⇇ ⇉

Twenty runners nervously toe the starting line.

Runners Set!

The gun's up.

Crack! Smoke! And we're off around the super-wide first turn under the scoreboard.

Someone takes a spill over the inside rail in the first 60m or so and they call us back to do it all over again. No one is hurt, which is good. But everybody is amped up. Skittish. More than before.

There's a reason they call the fenced-off area where they keep us before the race "the paddock." It's a horse racing term. And in many ways, the runners feel and act like the nervous thoroughbreds of the Triple Crown here. Energy all pent up and ready to spring at the sound of the gun.

Track season in my day was broken up into basically three parts.

Winter in New Jersey is a gray space. Sure, we get sun sometimes, but from October through the beginning of April, the clouds cover the blue more often than not. But as the temperatures start to turn, and any leftover snow plowed into the Kings Supermarket parking lot begins to melt into dingy gray water, spring track season comes into view.

That first week of March, usually March 7th, is the first team meeting. Everyone who wants to compete turns out. Boys, girls, all together. Bernards was a small school, just 140 or so in my graduating class. 600-some seventh through twelfth graders in the small campus along the Rockwellian residential street.

Mr. Mather makes one of his speeches to inspire us all. Demanding. Aspirational. Everyone believing in big things. Even the newbies. Mr. Ferry, Dandy Don, history teacher, Athletic Director (AD), gives us all the rules as he hands out our uniforms in exchange for permission slips. Gray sweats and white singlets. We cross-country guys and girls, keep our balloon suits if we're quiet about it and we almost always wear our own red shorts because the school-provided shorts look like, and wear like, they're from 1972.

The look on Mr. Ferry's face was alight with resentment towards us distance runners. We were the most successful team and athletes at the school when our other coaches and our serious A.D. wished beyond wish to have a dominant football program. Such was not in the cards for our little Group I school.

On top of that, they believed we didn't follow the rules. We got the same attitude from the New Jersey Interscholastic Athletic Association (NJSIAA) Officials. Resentment or jealousy, it seemed at the time. Either that or we were projecting. We may have been projecting some. But I was probably a biased teenager.

Be careful what you think you know about a person, because you're probably wrong. But that's a different, longer story.

The first week of March was anticipated by us. We'd trained hard all summer. Raced hard all fall through a hard-fought cross-country campaign. A disappointing finish for our Captain, Jim Nielsen. And a hard indoor season we tried our best to train through without draining the speed from ourselves for what challenges Spring would bring.

Not every state observes indoor track season, but indoor running was a thing for us. Just across the river from New York City where legends ran through smoking spectators and hacking dry coughs on the banked boards of Madison Square Garden at the Millrose Games every year, we went to watch from the nosebleed seats with 17,000 other track fans every February. Then we dreamed about it as we ran spikeless state championships at Jadwin Gymnasium on the Princeton campus or invitationals at West Point, or all comers meets on the bare, wooden floor of one of the Armories. New York. Jersey City.

Mark instructed us all to take two weeks "active rest" before the preparation for Relay season began. March 7th was the re-start when the snow started to melt and the temperatures transitioned us from indoor to outdoor track season—this is not the way it works everywhere in the country, but it is how things go in the Northeastern states.

The early meets were the relay meets, mainly designed to get the most participants involved. Track & Field is a sport where anybody who wants to participate, can, regardless of skill or ability. Relays offer an opportunity for four runners, jumpers, or throwers to compete together as a team. Somerset County Relays. Colonial Hills Conference Relays. Then the big meets that prep your team for Penn. The Rutgers Relays. The Colonial Relays in Virginia. The Father Judge Relays in Philly. All giving the most competitive teams a chance to try out their line-ups before the grand-daddy of them all inside Franklin Field on the last weekend in April.

The events that don't get run much. The Sprint Medleys. The four-bys. 4 x 200m, 4 x 800m, and the many, many mile relays. Four runners, four laps and a baton. Shuttle hurdles back and forth. Jumping and throwing relay teams.

And my favorite, the Distance Medley.

Villanova at the Penn Relays was like Babe Ruth and the Yankees in the World Series. The Wildcats sent men's teams that won a full 25% of the Distance Medley Championships of America in the 20th Century. Plus a long list of 4 x 800m, 4 x mile, sprint meds, 4 x 4s, and other events. So many Olympians, National Collegiate Athletic Association (NCAA) Champions. Mostly coached by James "Jumbo" Elliott, a card-carrying sport legend who only coached Villanova part-time as he ran his own construction equipment business around the Philadelphia region.

And they all cared about Penn more than anything else.

So to compete in that event, even the high school Championship of America, was to become a part of that long, storied history.

**APRIL 15, 1984. THE FATHER JUDGE RELAYS.**
**NINE DAYS BEFORE PENN. RAIN. WIND. ALL DAY.**

Thomas Augustine Judge was an American Catholic priest who organized a mission of lay people in the Northeast, specifically Philadelphia, through the earliest part of the 20th Century. As the population of the city boomed after World War II, the Diocese recognized the need for a new Catholic High School in the eastern reaches of the city that they named after Father Judge.

A highly ranked school, Father Judge produced several major league pitchers, a bishop, several prominent Pennsylvania politicos, a Pennsylvania Supreme Court Justice, an MMA Fighter and so we don't think they're perfect, Jeffrey Clark, lawyer indicted in connection with the effort to overturn the results of the 2020 Presidential Election.

But we were there for a track meet. In the rain. Less than two weeks before Penn.

Ninety minutes driving through the rain from Bernardsville to the east side of Philadelphia—and I started to understand W.C. Fields' epitaph —"I'd rather be here, than Philadelphia." Mark made a coaching decision and swapped up assignments. I ran Jim Nielsen's usual anchor leg while Jim took my 1,200m leg. Steve Patrick moved up to run a self-acknowledged uncomfortable 800m and Ranjan Sinha sat out this week resting a sore leg. Mark Strahs jumped in as our 400m man. The conditions slowed us down to a pedestrian 10:37, but we won by more than five seconds over Penn Charter surviving the brutal weather. I don't know what the splits were, but that was the day Clarence Dickerson started watching distance runners.

I don't know what it was about that day. It was cold, bitter, rainy, and very, very windy, but Clarence decided I was worth keeping an eye on to the point where two weeks later, inside Franklin Field, he felt the need to shout out encouragement from his VIP seat in the stands to a skinny, white, 14-year-old suburban New Jersey kid.

Known and loved by everyone as "The Chocolate Man," Clarence seemed to me after that to be everywhere. He was a coach at West Philadelphia and Bensalem High Schools. I don't remember exactly how I met him officially, myself, but I'm fairly certain that my dad was behind it. My dad was the mayor of wherever he went. He had a knack of easily getting to know everyone, particularly everyone who mattered. But one meet after another, I ended up spending time high up in the stands holding court with Choc. Coach after coach would come by to wave or have a word with him. All the big meets. ALL the big Philly meets. Young athletes would come to say hello as we chatted about the latest results. William Reed, the 400m phenom of the time was constantly in the conversation. They say he ran repeats with potato chips in his hands. If he could run fast without breaking the chips, it helped him run loose and relaxed. He'd ask me about Wetmore, who would become a friend, and how we trained and I'd ask him about sprinting and running fast. Eventually, he started coming over the Delaware River to see some of our meets in the Garden State and I enjoyed his insight and his friendship that always felt so unlikely. His entourage was almost entirely black and I came from the whitest distance running town in the country. And I'd get the jealous eye from some of his athletes wondering who this white guy was. But he always made it comfortable. It was just friends hanging at a track meet. And there's not much better in the world than that.

## FRIDAY, APRIL 27, 1984, 4:54 P.M.
## NINE DAYS LATER - THE RESTART.

Back inside Franklin Field. The fallen runner is back up and we're lined up again ready to restart the race. Twenty teams in a California stagger. 1200 meters that can't win the race, but can most certainly put your team in an inescapable hole. The gun goes off and we're racing. Elbows and spikes flying around the first turn all trying desperately to prove something to their coaches, their anchor men, their parents and their future college coaches. But mostly to themselves.

Two hundred and fifty meters in and the race starts defining itself. Tall, skinny, 14-year-old me had a shoulder on short, strong, very, very fast Tony DiGiovanni from Cranford. He'd won the indoor Meet of Champions 800m title at 1:53 and no one who knew anything about anything believed I could hold my own against somebody like that. My back kick was so high, I drew blood when I accidentally spiked him in the hand. The pack was crowded, two Jamaican teams, Vere Tech and St. Elizabeth, North Hunterdon from NJ, CBA, Mt. St. Michaels. Don't get me started on the parochial school team programs. It is Philadelphia after all.

I remember staring down the lane lines trying to stay in the moment of the race. I remember hearing the timer call out "Fifty-seven, fifty-eight, fifty-nine..." as we passed through the zone the first time. One of the Penn windbreaker officials calling splits. Then, hang onto Tony on the back stretch the second time around.

Slide around the far turn onto the short finishing straight to 800m together in 1:59, 2:00, 2:01.

Hang on tight, by the skin of my teeth through the next 200m. Everybody feels like they're carrying a piano down the back stretch.

Unwind from 200m out with everything we have left. Me step and step with Tony, who would later become a friend the way you do after a tough race. The others chasing us down close. Steve Patrick waiting for me to enter the zone so he could carry the stick on his turn around the oval.

We hit the exchange even, Tony maybe a half-step ahead. I wandered onto the bright green artificial turf of the infield to lie on my back, sucking oxygen out of the sunny South Philly air. Officially 3:04.3. Pete Carroll had me at 3:03.8, so that's what I choose to remember. But none of that mattered at the time. Or now. Sidebar stories. All of it. I forced myself to stand in time to watch Steve-O hand off to Ranjan, the other sophomore on the team.

One minute and fifty-eight seconds later, he dropped the stick into Jim Nielsen's fist about ten or twelve meters down on Bill Barrett of CBA. Jim caught him in lap 1. Passed him in lap 2. And ran away from the field in 4:13 for a team 10:06.09.

The watch. The wheel. the celebration. The decision on the next race. The 4 x 800m.

We warmed down, jogging around the city blocks surrounding the stadium all lined with booths selling t-shirts, and food and other Philadelphia paraphernalia, our meet credentials dangling from the zippers at our necks. It truly was the carnival that I didn't fully realize until after the buzz of race preparation was over. We ate funnel cakes in the stands and watched the last few big races of the day. We decided that we would not get up early for the 4 x 800m trials in the morning. One victory was enough for this Penn experience. The 4 x 8 would require two races on Saturday A full effort trial early in the morning just for a chance to make the afternoon final. Then a bigger effort Saturday afternoon against so many fresh-legged runners from all over the country and Jamaica for just a chance at a second Championship of America. Two untested sophomores, the great Jim Nielsen and a player to be named later trying to compete with a championship field ready to run 7:45? Possible, sure. But unlikely. Mark may have been a little disappointed in the moment, but it was a good decision with a long season to come.

    We all went out to dinner to celebrate. The coaches as happy as we'd ever seen them. Mark and Joe Laspada, the girls coach, who graduated together and Mr. Mather who was in his celebratory element, all smiles, stories, and bragging rights. All of us walking up and around the corner and along Chestnut St. from the Sheraton University City. We sat in a restaurant laughing and goofing around. Jim hanging a spoon on his nose and Ranjan being embarrassed. Parents and the boys all smiling and silly together. The girls 4 x 800 team who ran on Thursday at the next table, giggling. Then, the next day, we sat in the north stands experiencing Saturday at the Carnival and watching Irishman John McDonnell's Arkansas Razorbacks establish themselves as the heirs to Jumbo Elliott's Villanova crown. A trend that would last a decade as we considered, "how far is Little Rock from here?"

# The Beginning

# 3

"The mind is not a vessel that needs filling,
but wood that needs igniting."

- Plutarch

I remember running the "novice" meet somewhere in Morris County. I think it was at Randolph. I also remember learning the meaning of the word "novice."

I sprinted. I long jumped. I thought the shot was too heavy to do anyone any good. And somebody, I think it was Bob Jones who would later become my geometry teacher, who I'd find out had a silver Penn Relays watch from the IC4A mile relay when he was at Manhattan College; but it was Bob Jones, I think, who put me in the Novice Mile. I have no record of what the time was. Whether it was fast or slow. Probably slow. I'd never raced a mile before.

I don't remember what shoes I ran in, or what shorts. Probably blue Adidas suede kicks with long, white tube socks and orange stripes around the tops. I do remember running races in a red Bernardsville Recreation t-shirt just like everybody else. Different colors. Different town names. Randolph was blue. Dark. Ridge was green, because of course, the Red Devils.

Four whole laps. I was petrified before the race began, but took the chance anyway and ran fourth in the race and had nothing but internal confidence after that. I was about 10.

I first met Mark Wetmore after that. It was 1979 and the running boom was at its peak boominess. Somewhere at a meet with a 220-yard concrete track on a grassy hill. I think Paul Stogryn was there, and maybe Mike Flood. Some of the guys I'd come to know so well later. I remember being very nervous like I was meeting somebody important. Turns out I was. At least someone who would be important to me.

My dad took me over to the hill on one end of the little blacktop oval. Sitting on the lawn with a group of other people was this guy. He was so serious and intimidating. Tall compared to me. And slim with a hawk nose and long-ish brown hair. He reached out to shake my hand.

"Call me Mark."

And I never called him anything else.

I stood there for a few minutes as my dad talked to him. And I answered some of his basic questions. I wish I remembered more of what we said, but I was scared and nervous and unsure, but something about him made me excited about the future and what might be possible for me. The reputation of the Bernards team preceded itself.

Then my mind skips forward to training summer on Claremont Rd. with Mrs. Knox. The young kids ran with some of the moms, keeping us safe on the mean streets of Bernardsville.

# WORKOUT: Rolling Hill Rd.

Anyone who's studied Arthur Lydiard even a little bit will be familiar with his hill workouts. Springing. Bounding. Sprints, etc. Lydiard was instilled in my mind as a legend of the same caliber as Arthur Pendragon, Robin Hood, Atlantis and Lady Godiva. Something so very important and critical to understanding humanity, but so mysterious to so many that it may not have actually existed at all in the first place.

I remember doing my first true Lydiard-style hill workout in the early fall when I was about 11-years-old. I was introduced to a lot of these things when I was about 11. The whole crowd jogged over Old Fort Road toward the Polo Grounds, but stopped a bit short at Rolling Hill Road. It was where my neighbor, Mrs. Bierbauer served as crossing guard every morning and afternoon when school was in session. She was gone at this time of the day and the traffic was gone, too, so twenty or more of us jogged to the bottom of the hill.

Mark described the workout, which would be 12 repeats of the hill. Not running fast. At all. We should spring up as high as we could on each step and slowly work our way up the steep hill that was about 200m in horizontal distance.

When we started, we had to learn how it all felt. Most of us started skipping and had to be corrected into basically a running in place form, then drive up into the sky. Meet your right hand to your chin, then drive the right knee up and the left hand to the chin. Then repeat. Slowly. Working your way up the hill. One springing step at a time.

No stopwatch. No speed. Just tag the phone pole at the top of the hill, turn and jog back down for the next one.

12 times.

## MT. KENYA

Years later, the hills had evolved. Mark found a narrow little trail in the thick trees between Hardscrabble Road and Crest Drive. Then a little trail back down to Chestnut on the back side of the Polo Grounds.

I don't know how he found these trails or how hard he orienteered his way around Bernardsville in those days, but Mark always found the perfect place to do the workout he had in mind. Mt. Kenya was a narrow, straight, steep hill where we did springing, then bounding a few times each fall to get strong for the racing season. It was a version of the Lydiard hills, but different, too. We'd each pick up a pair of stones - equal in weight and as heavy as we thought we could manage. Then 8-10 springing repeats. Then 8-10 bounding repeats up the hill. We'd all jog down between each one widening the trail as we went. We were back far enough in the woods that none of the houses could see the steady loop of 25+ runners, but the people in those homes started to notice us as we jogged back up and over and out of the trail back onto the road to the school at the end.

The hills took all the long distance base training we did over the summer and start to convert it into useable strength. We hated it. And we loved it.

# Run-for-Fun

# 4

> "People in small towns, much more than in cities, share a destiny."
>
> - Richard Russo

It was a hand-drawn flyer posted on the wall of the school that grabbed my attention. One of those blue mimeograph sheets that stained your fingers all through grammar school.

RUN-4-FUN!

I wasn't sure exactly what it was, but I knew my dad ran hurdles in school. And I was always fascinated by the concentric lane lines on the track I could see from the car window as we drove through town to Nardone's Bakery after church on Sunday. The view was downhill over the green grass past the grandstands onto the black track surface with the white lines painted on it. I thought it looked like an Olympic Stadium at the time. I was so small and it was so big. Of course, it wasn't really. But it sure seemed so. Emily didn't care. My sister was a year younger than me and already in ballet classes, so maybe that was it. She had her thing already even at that young age. I just wanted my own thing that didn't require me to wait for her classes to be done in the lobby of a rehearsal hall inside the Essex Building on Claremont Road every other night of the week.

It would be a few years before the Basset Ballet Company brought Adriana Dometresciu from Ukraine in to teach the young girls. Mostly girls. I took classes for a time but not long. Marched as a tin soldier in The Nutcracker. Twice. Another brainstorm of my mothers, getting me into ballet class. As if telling me all the pro football teams were doing it would somehow make it better.

So many of those girls went on to the New Jersey Ballet, and American Ballet Theater in New York City, then Lisa Kreutz on to the Kirov in St. Petersburg. I was always proud of my sister's talent. She may not know or have known, or ever believed me at the time. There's probably another book in just that experience.

I was rushed to the hospital as a very young child in the midst of an anaphylactic reaction. Twice.

I had a surprise allergic reaction to something and the passages in my lungs narrowed suddenly blocking my ability to breathe. I was rushed to the emergency room for an immediate injection of something, benadryl? epinephrine? adrenaline? Whatever the treatment was at the time to reverse the effect of the allergic reaction.

As you're reading this here, you know I survived, so no cliffhanger there. I was so young I don't really remember the experience. Either time.

The standard allergy testing revealed, gratefully, I wasn't allergic to any foods or medications, but I was pretty severely allergic to just about anything you could breathe.

My parents took me to an allergy specialist in Philadelphia. Dr. Wood gave me an extensive scratch test to see what I reacted to. I remember the test was a grid over my entire back and we had to wait a few minutes to see which allergens reacted and chart them all. I remember two things from that trip. Sitting in traffic along the Schuylkill Expressway in the summer heat and learning I was at least somewhat allergic to something I could breathe in each and every season of the year. I was diagnosed as a borderline chronic asthmatic and set up for a long series of desensitization shots. Something Dr. Wood was at the forefront of developing at the time. Two shots of a serum developed from my own sputum, twice a week. We started by making twice-weekly appointments at the allergist, but eventually, my mom would just take me over to our neighbor, Mrs. Becker, who was a nurse to get the shots.

The standard treatment for asthma, chronic asthma, when I was young was total rest. All the doctors believed in it. They thought any excess irritation from heavy breathing would throw their young patients, especially, into an asthmatic reaction and risk serious damage or worse.

Dr. Wood went the other way. His radical idea of the time was for patients like me to get involved in as much exercise as I could tolerate to strengthen the diaphragm and musculature supporting the lungs and counteract the effects of any potential asthma attack.

Of course, he was right.

Over time, I started to get chronic ear infections as a kid. I had tubes put in my ears more than once. And in the summertime, I wasn't allowed to swim with them. A local allergist told my mom I could swim if she packed my ears with lamb's wool and I wore a swim cap. We tried it. And I looked oh, so cool. They were already making fun of the way I walked. Add to that discovering I was allergic to lamb's wool and swimming was an absolute terror for me.

With all the visits to the allergist and the shots and the tubes and the lamb's wool debacle, I could have felt like a sickly kid. I probably should have felt like the weird, geeky, sickly kid, but with Dr. Wood's advice on exercise, we began to look for any dry-land athletic endeavor we could find. My dad entered me in every sport I had any interest in even if he didn't. Any sport I wanted, even if I didn't show any aptitude.

Run-4-Fun. My dad saw the same notice in the Bernardsville News along with a little article, tacked on the bulletin board of the library. The informational meeting would be in the High School Auditorium.

I'd already been there for...

Little League—couldn't catch, couldn't throw, hit by a pitch or two. Quit end of season.

Basketball—Coach spent too much time trying to explain the 3-second lane violation and I lost understanding of the whole game. Quit.

Flag Football—I was fast, but couldn't catch. Thought the rules were too complicated.

Soccer—loved it. And Pele. Was competent, but not great. Forced eventually to choose.

But this was different.

We sat in the audience with everybody else. Then this guy appeared on the stage with a microphone. Dynamic. Funny. Massive presence on a slim distance runner's frame. I got the impression he was a teacher at the school but he was a force of nature as he described what running was all about. The fun. The excitement.

That was Ed Mather. The one and only Phineas T. Barnum of track & field. How important he made it all sound as he spoke and told stories. Heroic. And there would be other kids. I liked the sound of that. I wanted some friends.

I'd been made fun of unmercifully for the way I walked from a very early age. I bounced on my toes almost floating along. I never thought about it because I couldn't see it. But walking along the sidewalk outside the middle school, a bunch of the other boys walked behind me mocking the bounce without mercy. Laughing at me and encouraging others to join in. It made me feel silly. Different. Unwanted. Weird. My mom even took me to my pediatrician, Dr. Taylor, when I was small to try and find a solution. He said my hamstrings were tight or my achilles tendons were tight and the only thing he could suggest was wearing heavy shoes. So my mom bought me heavy dress shoes and insisted that I wear them every day. That did not help the physical issue of bouncing. Or my social status. And you can only imagine how it helped the bullying situation. But that was my mom. Always trying to do the right thing without thinking about consequences.

Mr. Mather was still on stage talking. Telling stories about the great runners of the Bernards High School Pack. That's what they called the cross-country team because they all ran and raced together. He brought a few of his high school champions on stage with him. He talked about what we'd need (and it wasn't much). A pair of shoes if we didn't have them already. And we could get a discount at the Sneaker Barn in Chester. Ten percent off! It was great! Shorts. We'd all get a t-shirt. That red Bernardsville Recreation t-shirt I wore for so long until it was more holes than shirt.

A couple of evenings a week—voluntary. Dozens of kids turned out to run laps on the track, shuttle relays, baton passing. We long-jumped into the sand. We high-jumped into the soft pits. We threw the very heavy shot put with help. We started to learn the lingo. And we hung out and laughed and played on the school fields getting to know each other.

We were coached by some of the High School teachers. It's where I first met Bob Jones. Dozens of kids all from the same small town. Some I knew. More I'd know later.

And some of the high schoolers "coached" us little kids making sure nobody got hurt. They were like heroes to us. Bigger than life thanks to the never-ceasing commentary of Coach Ed Mather. Always running everywhere. All over the field. Sometimes with his dog in tow. Acting the part of the ringmaster making sure we were all having a great time. Smiling. Laughing. Thinking bigger things like getting a spot on the cross-country team was the greatest honor this side of the Nobel Prize.

Years later, I realized what the purpose of this program was. A feeder system into the high school team. Not recruiting. Just a way of introducing us to all sides of the sport and getting at least some of us excited to be a part of something bigger.

We ALL loved it. And those of us who had some success, kept going. And the best of us started running together every day. And we became part of The Pack. The Long Red Line. The legend loomed large.

## THE BERNARDS MOUNTAINEERS

**Boys XC**—23 state championships, 14 consecutive. 199 consecutive dual meets. 3 All-Group championship teams.

**Girls XC**—12 state championships, 10 consecutive. 1 All-Group championship team.

Easterns. Invitationals. Track Championships. Penn Relays. 129 Individual boys state champions in track & XC. 91 Girls.

All from a school of just more than 600 kids.

It felt like being a part of the '27 Yankees. There was nothing else like it.

## THE MINE MOUNTAIN ROAD DEPARTMENT

Soon after, it was Spring and school was still in session. I didn't understand what it was all about at the time, but my dad, it was always my dad, took me to a meeting in the basement cafeteria of St. Elizabeth's School on Seney Drive in Bernardsville. It was our parish. Just down the street from the house. We drove there in my dad's 1977 VW Rabbit. We could have walked.

This was an official meeting of the Mine Mountain Road Department. The running club that matured out of the Bernardsville Recreation Run-4-Fun program.

A couple of dozen people were there in the mostly quiet room when we arrived. A few of my fellow new runner kids and a few older kids I didn't know but saw around. Their parents, most I didn't know either. Mark was there with another, at the time intimidating figure. I'd come to know Larry Sullivan well later and over the years. I could name a bunch of the others, but I might not be right. There was a diminutive woman with a large personality and bright red hair at the front. Mrs. Grozier cut an outsized presence in the room. President of the new Mine Mountain Road Department running club, I would come to know her and her son, John, and all of the people in this room later. Some very well. I'm sure Rick Knox was there. I'm sure Mr. and Mrs. Beckwith were there. Mr. and Mrs. Hinman with Mike and Tracey. Mrs. Grozier was a mom, many of whom kept organizations like the MMRD running only because they loved and supported their children and their interests.

I'd never been to a meeting like that before. There were motions and seconds and votes and committee assignments and talk of a trip to something called "Millrose." Lots of things I didn't understand. My first exposure to Roberts Rules of Order and my dad gave somebody a check and I was handed my first Mine Mountain Road Department singlet with black Dolphin shorts. Bright yellow mesh with a black double M in the shape of runners on the chest. On the back, a big orange triangle indicating a slow-moving vehicle. They were great shorts, but did not have a brief inside which became an issue very quickly. What do you wear under these things?

This group became in many ways, a new part of my family. The club, my home for the next several years and beyond.

Most running clubs at the time were "harriers" (cross-country runners), or "striders," or an "A.C." (athletic club). Some were just named "the town name runners" and some were clever like "Fleet Feet." Later, we'd always say snidely, not knowing any of them, "they don't look that fleet to me." Unfair and childish, but we were children.

Most were open to participants from all over their region. Multiple schools. Multiple towns. People who didn't know each other. Only recognized the uniforms. They didn't train together. Much. They only turned up at the races listed on the sheet.

Mine Mountain Road Department was different. It was born out of a small town. And we all trained together. Everybody was headed to the same high school. We knew each other. And came to love spending time together under a common purpose.

They got our name wrong in the paper all the time. But that only meant we were in the paper all the time. The Mine Mountain Road Running Club. The Mine Mt. Running Track Team. The Mine Brook Runners. The Bernardsville Mountain Road Running Track Team. And everything in between. We didn't mind so much. We always felt different from everyone else so why wouldn't they miss the name. They never missed the black and yellow uniforms going by them.

The team—club—existed in a way about a year, maybe more, before I was invited to join. It was still a sort of an extension of the Run-for-Fun Recreation Commission group. At least that's where most of the kids grew into it from. Eventually, the yellow singlets and black shorts would take over from the red t-shirts, but in 1978, a small team from a small town in little New Jersey qualified and traveled together out to Kansas City to compete in the AAU Junior Olympic Cross Country Nationals. This was one of the first stories I ever heard. One of the many to become legend.

Mike Hinman, his sister Tracey, Brad Hudson, Tim Peters, John Grozier, Chris Blanchet, Meg Waldron, and George Swain all qualified to compete and they raised funds for the trip selling brownies in town. Eventually, the MMRD grew to compete in all sorts of events junior to masters, kids to parents, all over the country together.

I remember hearing at my first MMRD meeting that the nationals were in New Jersey that year. Somewhere called the Peddie School. So the Jersey kids wouldn't be required to run a "regional" qualifier. We'd go straight from the states to the Nationals. That helped us grow as a team, too. Nearby Heightstown made it easy to get there as a spectator. No travel expenses meant more kids. Growth opportunity for all the New Jersey clubs like the Hunterdon Harriers and the Shore A.C.

It was frigid and windy on the Peddie Golf Course when race day came. I remember feeling the cold air in and out of my lungs as I tried to keep up. I was back in the field but there were a few high finishers from our team. My first "big race" experience.

The MMRD ran well. We were now a club people knew and one to be watched as we grew into our own.

# Tears & Time Trials

# 5

"Our chief want in life is somebody who will make us do what we can."

- Ralph Waldo Emerson

**OCTOBER, 1979.**

**SIXTH GRADE. 10 YEARS OLD.**

When I found out, I just about ran all the way home. Dressed for school. Red nylon Bernardsville Eagles bag bouncing off my shoulder the whole way. I just about sprinted past Mrs. Bierbauer, my next door neighbor and our crossing guard on Seney Drive. I clambered up the big hill of Stevens Street and into the house. Up the stairs to my room where I decided was the best place to hide out. The tears came streaming from my eyes from a place of deep, deep fear.

I still can't really explain it and it's a story I don't think I've ever told anyone. One of those incredibly embarrassing moments you can't outlive in your own head even though you know you were just a kid.

I couldn't tell you what it was that flipped the switch in my heart. What was different this time. I'd run races before. In my red Rec t-shirt. I'd run and hung out with most of the people running in THIS race almost every day. But when Pete Beckwith asked me at the end of the school day if I was ready for the meet, I just said "what meet?"

I had no memory of it on the calendar. I'm still bad with the calendar. Just ask my wife, Heather, how good I am with dates. It was Friday. Just a light run and then home most weeks. I didn't expect much from Mark other than a beautiful Fall day on the Polo Grounds.

But today, there were buses in the parking lot with kids from other schools spilling out to warm up. In uniforms I'd never seen before. The view of it all frightened me deeply. And I ran. No apology. No explanation. Just ran the one mile to my bedroom.

I didn't know I was supposed to race that day. My first with Mark as my coach.

The first. With Mark.

Aha.

And I couldn't do it. I cried and I hid my face.

Mom had no idea what was wrong. But she managed to get me to come down to the kitchen table to tell her what was bothering me. Cliche, I know, but the brown formica kitchen table was where all of our important conversations and family moments happened. I'm sure to this day she didn't understand what was so traumatic to me.

"There's a race... and I can't..." was all I could manage to get out of my vibrating yawp. And mom wasn't going to push me. Never one to stretch out past the comfort zone that way.

The plain white van pulled up in front of the house. Our kitchen window looked out over the front yard at the top of the hill onto our suburban street. It was Mark, coming to see what happened to me. I didn't know he knew where we lived. But small towns, I guess.

Mom went out and talked to my coach for a minute then pushed me out the front door to talk to him for myself. Through wet, swollen eyes, I told him what I knew, which wasn't really explicable for a 10-year-old. He listened. And spoke to me calmly as if there was nowhere else in the world he needed to be. Even though there was a cross-country meet he was in charge of just about to start a mile away.

Looking back on it, Mark was just 25 or 26, himself. Living at home in his family home. Teaching high school English. Coaching a young band of enthusiastic small-town kids.

I was set to race in the elementary field of the Bernards Invitational a week later. I didn't know there was a meet today. I was absolutely petrified. Completely surprised and irrational. There couldn't have been more than a couple of dozen boys in the race. Hardly anybody coming to cheer us on, time us, or direct traffic. But as soon as I heard "race," I was out. There was nothing I could tell Mark that made any sense. But he listened and somehow calmed me down. I looked out the windshield of the van down the steep hill of Stevens Street, the blue sky, fluffy clouds, and dark green canopy of oaks over the lawns. I tried to slow down, and listen, and breathe.

"How many of the other guys have I seen just like this?" he asked me letting the question float in the air. "All of them."

Of course I was trying to picture Paul Storgryn or Chris Blanchet sitting in my same position.

"Really?"

And I believed him. I still don't know if I was the only runner he ever had to chase down at home too scared to run, but it helped. Somehow, he convinced me I would be ok. That I was prepared. All the training I'd done with Mrs. Knox and Pete and Tom Beckwith and the others out on

Short Morning and Long Morning had me in good shape to climb up and down the hills and around the loops of the course. He never touched me. Patted me on the back or shoulder. Shook my hand. Hugging? No way. But something in his words and the tone of his voice—maybe just his confidence and a sense that he wanted to see what I was capable of got me to say "oooh kay."

I must have told mom what we were doing but I only remember Mark driving the white van back down Stevens Street to Claremont then a right turn through the five-point intersection past the churches and up Seney Dr. to the pool road that led to the gravel parking lot of the Polo Grounds.

I must have warmed up, but I don't remember that part either. I stood on the chalk line that extended out between the foul poles of two different baseball diamonds and waited for the crack of the gun. And in a blip—we were off. The crowd of boys in shorts and team t-shirts from Somerset and Morris County, New Jersey—Morristown kids and Basking Ridge kids. Black kids who we didn't see too many of in Bernardsville in those days, and white kids. Tall kids and short kids. Shaggy haired kids like my friend Pete. Kids a couple of years older to kids maybe a year younger than me. All racing together up and around the Pop Warner field. Down along the snow fence and up the wooded trail to Chestnut Road. I was excited and breathing hard but not overwhelmed. I was surprised to have so few people in front of me as we made the turn down Seney Drive. Mark was there shouting encouragement and instructions from the inside of the turn. We Bernardsville kids let our legs turn over and over and over down the hill to the left onto "Seney Extension," a private road we youngsters were taught to call "Agony Hill." But up we sailed to the trail turn onto the sweeping downhill where we could see the finish line. Coaches and a few parents waiting and shouting the names of their kids from the massive grassy field.

It was only a mile and a half, our course, half the distance of the varsity course, but it felt very important to me. I felt as if I'd fall on my face coming down the last hill if I didn't keep my feet racing to catch up with my body. As we all rushed toward the finish, I sprinted the best I could and crossed the line in fourth place, just behind Pete and Tom. Fourth place! I felt deep relief. And success. I liked it. I felt as good as if I'd won. And even at that young age, it felt like an important moment in my life. One that I'd remember and dream on later. And if Mark hadn't been there—I know I would have given up, scared, and probably would never have run another step.

parents waiting and shouting the names of their kids from the massive grassy field.

It was only a mile and a half, our course, half the distance of the varsity course, but it felt very important to me. I felt as if I'd fall on my face coming down the last hill if I didn't keep my feet racing to catch up with my body. As we all rushed toward the finish, I sprinted the best I could and crossed the line in fourth place, just behind Pete and Tom. Fourth place! I felt deep relief. And success. I liked it. I felt as good as if I'd won. And even at that young age, it felt like an important moment in my life. One that I'd remember and dream on later. And if Mark hadn't been there—I know I would have given up, scared, and probably would never have run another step.

# The day I met Hallinan

## 6

*"If I have seen further it is by standing on the shoulders of giants."*

- Isaac Newton

We all had different, unique experiences as young runners in Bernardsville. We got to know each other as peers and friends. Then we got to know some of those who came before and they inspired us to be a part of it all. To live in a small town is not necessarily to live in a place where everybody knows everybody, but just about everyone you know is connected in ways you don't always see right away.

I often ended up staying late, warming down with Mark as the sun went down. A couple of extra miles at the end in sweats. Others were only there when the whole team was there. The girls had their own different experiences together, usually as a group, giggling, joking, happy.

Some, like Brad Hudson, spent a ton of extra time running solo or with friends in Hunterdon like Andy Martin.

And that went on for all of us from a very young age running together after school and on the weekends and all over our small towns until we were old enough to drive. And then we drove to practice. Together. Always together.

One day late in the fall my first year, after the time change so it was getting dark, we'd finished our workout at the Polo Grounds. It was damp and getting cold. I was the last one there with Mark and we jogged up the Pool Road toward the Middle School where we linked up at random with this guy. Tall and fit and dressed in a beautiful, blue matching track suit. Mark knew him and introduced me—Chris. He and Mark chatted as we ran down Seney Drive. Chris asked me questions like I was a peer. Just another runner. Not some 11-year-old twerp. Like I was somebody he wanted to talk to. Mark and I turned up the hill on Seney Extension as this strong, smooth-strided runner headed up Old Fort Road back into the Autumn sunset toward somewhere I couldn't imagine. History, I supposed.

"That's Chris Hallinan. Best runner ever from here," Mark said. He told me he ran at Arizona State University, which sounded exotic to me at the time. I'd never even envisioned Arizona before. Not knowing what to say and weak to the power of nostalgia, I let it hang there in the misty air of October. It felt to me what it must be meeting Babe Ruth or Wilt Chamberlain. And I wanted to be like him.

I sat down to talk with Alex Cuesta and Dave Hyatt of the Talking in Ovals podcast. They know and love the sport and know and love NJ track history about as much as anyone. Their mission is to share their joy and enthusiasm for the sport. They had a vague notion of the success the Bernards team had at one time, but coming out of the 90s as they do, when I started telling stories, they didn't have the full picture.

Ed Mather came to Bernards High School o teach and coach in 1964. In 1979, the team was featured in the New York Times for just having won its 100th consecutive dual meet in boys cross-country. The

Pack, as the team was known at that time would continue the streak for another ten years to 199 straight dual meet victories. During that time, the team amassed 23 state cross-country team titles—14 in a row from 1973-1987, and three Meet of Champions titles in 1981, 1982, and 1985. It's the best record of any public school in New Jersey by far.

Add the girls team to that and you have 12 more state group titles—10 in a row from 1979-1986 and another Meet of Champions title in 1982—first time boys and girls teams from the same school accomplished the feat, ever. North Hunterdon would replicate the success the next year and no school has accomplished it since.

On the track, the story is similar. Personally, I won 8 individual group titles, 4 Meet of Champions titles. Add 4 state indoor relay titles and that's 16 total. John Carlotti had one group title before moving to Bernards from Cedar Grove, but then added his own 8 individual Group titles and five Meet of Champions titles indoors, outdoors and his cross-country win at Holmdel in 1982. Add one state indoor relays title and that's 15. That's just the two of us. Chris Hallinan captured ten individual titles on his own.

Three Penn Relays Distance Medley Championships of America in 1979, 1984, and 1986, plus innumerable other invitationals, sectionals, conference, counties, post-season. Add the MMRD to that in Junior Olympics, road racing, and records like Buck Logan's 8:52 two-mile run and longer distance performances from the likes Chris Hallinan and the record is substantial and honestly easy to lose track of. Not to mention the tangential success of people like Brad Hudson, who trained with us for years as a junior runner, who won the '83 NJSIAA Meet of Champions and finished second to Carlotti in '82. He moved to Oregon after that where he finished high school, ran at the University of Oregon and became a world-class coach himself. All that belongs to Brad, of course, but I think Bernardsville gets to claim a small brag, too. The history of running in Bernardsville can, frankly, be overwhelming.

I always knew what I was experiencing in Bernardsville running was different. Something unique compared to the other teams in the state—maybe—probably anywhere.

I think maybe it's my son Aiden who finally got me to start writing the stories down. When you have a smart, curious kid, he asks a lot of questions you're not prepared to answer in the moment. And you have to answer them honestly. They know when you don't. So I started telling him the story. Stories. And he had an interest in joining the team at his school—I hope it's not just because of me. Heather ran track. Sprints and hurdles at Middletown South. But she did other things, too. Leads in the plays and musicals. Cheerleading and majorette. She was a better student than I was. The multiple advanced degrees are evidence to that.

But he asks and I tell him. I think it's important for him to know what it was like during the running boom. For us. Maybe its important for you to know, too.

There are schools who had people go on to run at a very high level—scholarships and professionals. Olympians and beyond. As I write this, I'm taking my son, Aiden, to an "Elise Cranny Race Watch Party" today at Niwot High School. She's a Niwot and Stanford grad and running the

5,000m final in Paris hoping to give a medal a run. She still trains here and people on his team still know her and her family.

Mark Wetmore—Aiden met him at a couple of meets this year—has had many national champions and Olympians under his guidance. Great and significant coaches, too. But I feel like there's something else about the Bernardsville story that goes missing sometimes.

Arthur Lydiard famously said there are champions walking all around us. They just need to be trained properly.

And I think that's what sticks with me. And not in the way it stuck with the characters in the film "That Championship Season" where they all got stuck. Arrested in a sense of adolescent self-importance and artificially boosted ego.

Something else. Something familial. Something good.

When we run into each other, we hardly ever talk about the championships or races or trophies or medals or wins. We talk about our families and then we remember all the time we spent together, just hanging out and being human together. Then we remember the workouts and the trails and mud and rain and snow. The bus rides and goofy moments in the stands. The pain and euphoria of the 12th repeat up Mount Kenya. The time I could practically reach out and touch Carlo between the shoulder blades as he just stepped by me on that winter 1,500m time trial when I was a freshman. Mike Hinman working so hard to break 2:00 that he thew up at the top of the last straightaway. Twice.

The intensity our first man, Jim Nielsen, had on the small bus Mr. Mather drove to Van Cortlandt Park for the Easterns in 1984 and how we didn't understand where it came from. And how we all wanted to do something to help him, but couldn't figure out what or how.

Pete Carroll driving us to the Warren Raquet Club to lift weights all summer in his old, red, VW Beetle. Getting to be friends with him and his experiences at Villanova. He gave me John Marshall's spikes to race in and I ran in them until they fell apart. And Buck Logan who ran 8:52 and John Sullivan who ran 3:00 at Penn. They'd been through what you're going through and made you feel good about it even though you never talked about it directly.

They inspired just by being who they were.

Family by choice. In generations. In all the best ways and none of the worst.

One day as high schoolers, in gym class, we were doing a golf unit getting ready to hit balls aimlessly into a net set up in the wrestling room. Jesse Taylor was instructing us. Jesse was a classic, old-school gym teacher. Military vet with tattoos he hid from us under long sleeves and a regular sneer designed to keep us all in line. He was a starter for the New Jersey State Interscholastic Athletic Association (NJSIAA) and we got to know him that way standing out in front of a stampede of boys and girls in shorts on the flat field of The Polo Grounds every fall.

"Gentlemen, doff your sweats!" he'd shout in an effort to be entertaining while moving the meet along.

We got to know him a little better at a race in Lewis Morris Park once. He was good friends with Ed Carroll, Pete's dad. And Ed Carroll was absolutely beloved. So if Ed liked Jesse, he must be ok. We all chatted for a long while after that race in the State Park in Morristown that bordered and shared trees with Jockey Hollow, the national park where Ed worked and Pete grew up. From that point on, I saw Jesse's act for what it was. A put-on. His soft, kind eyes betrayed him.

"Simpson!" he shouted out echoing to the other end of the wrestling room. Jeff and Pete Beckwith and I were talking, telling stories and jokes the way we always did. Jesse picked out Jeff for some reason. He could have picked on any of us runners.

"Do you want to hit golf balls or would you rather run laps for the rest of class?"

We quieted down and Jesse turned toward some of the other, better-behaved students, at which point, Jeff shrugged his shoulders, got up, and jogged out the door of the lower gym up the stairs to the track.

"Where's Simpson?" he asked when he finally got back to us toward the end of the class.

"You asked if he'd rather run laps."

An angry grimace crossed the man's face as he shook his head in exasperation—but I was sure he smiled as he dismissed us all back to the locker room.

Social media makes it easier to keep in touch and up to date with what's new with all these people. At least on a surfacey level.

Friend and teammate, Jenny Rahn, asked a question on Facebook yesterday about the finish of the men's Olympic 100m dash final. Why the standard is the torso and not the toes? Or any other body part crossing the line? There was some thoughtful, some humorous commentary until

Hallinan knocked it out of the park, saying "probably because the chest contains the heart."

Wherever I see Hallinan's name cross my screen, I'm instantly 11 years old again. And when he says something like that, I'm instantly in a mental space of growing into something important. Deep. My sense of wonder is activated and I am that little kid with big dreams trotting next to Wetmore and, Chris Hallinan, the best runner my town ever produced. I'm the kid who just caught a Willie Mays home run. The 56-year-old man melts away.

I never knew Chris well, at least I never thought so, but we crossed paths with frequency after that first chance run together. At the Asbury Park Boardwalk races. The Utica Boilermaker trips. The Midland Run. Summer training at the wall. And he always talked to me like I was a peer. That same way he did that first cold fall day—even though I was ten years younger and he was my age the day I was born. A friend. And that means everything.

It's Friday afternoon on the last weekend of April in 1983 and I'm getting sunburned in the direct rays of the East Stands of Franklin Field about 120m from the finish line. There's a bunch of us. My dad to my left talking to one of the other parents. I'm there just as a spectator. I'd been to Millrose at the Garden and Vitalis at the Meadowlands. We went to cheer on the team at the relays in Rutgers Stadium and the Meet of Champions in Palmer Stadium at Princeton last spring. My dad brought me to the IC4As at Jadwin in the winter and I smelled the liniment on the breeze and saw the Villanova guys race, but I'd never seen anything like this. Felt, smelled, experienced anything like this.

Forty thousand people in a stadium cheering on college and high school relays. You could forgive me for thinking every track meet was like this. My friends would be stepping onto the track in a few minutes.

I knew our guys won back in '79. The Championship of America. So I thought it was a regular thing. I was as confident in that as anything I'd ever been.

Then, standing on the red and blue colored bleachers, I spotted a flash of bright, white sneakers next to me. Painfully bright, white, leather K-Swiss with metal eyelets, blue jeans, a striped canvas belt, pink Oxford shirt buttoned at the cuffs and round, brown lensed shades. Smiling softly under unfairly good hair, it was the first time I'd seen Hallinan in street clothes. He was there for the same reason I was—The High School Boys Distance Medley. And there was Pete Carroll, sitting on the other side and Mark sitting rows back, watching, assessing, waiting the way he always did. Mr. Mather was holding court on the aisle. Maybe the anxiety of the moment had him talking more than normal. Maybe it was just him. The girls team that already won the 4 x 800m Championship were sitting around—Meg and Jenny and Tasha and Amy. And Jodi McCain and others on the team and parents and friends all around us there on the turn by the steeplechase pit.

We followed the schedule in the thick Penn program. JP who I'd already run an exceedingly long number of miles with was there—JP, who I'd run a lifetime of miles more before we were done.

Then, 4:50 p.m., we spotted Paul Stogryn dart out of the paddock in all white, special uniforms for a special event. Something else to irritate our Athletic Director, "Dandy" Don Ferry and the BHS administration. Knocking out the nerves with a few strides before being called to the line.

The order was different than '79. Charlie Wade led off at 800m that year and John Sullivan insisted that's the only reason he ran as fast a 1200m as he did. Third leg gave them running room and that's why no one would ever run three-flat again, he said.

In a moment, they were all lined up, poised and tense for the release of the gun.

And they were off. Twenty leadoff men from 20 high school teams from all over the country and Jamaica.

Stogryn handed off to Sean Tutton, normally a soccer star, to carry the next 400m. Not known for our sprinters, Tutton battled the faster guys from the sprint schools valiantly and handed off to Chris Blanchet for a quick two-lapper to put us back in the hunt.

John Carlotti took it from there. Known for his 800m speed, "Carlo" staked out ground as a cross-country champion in the fall, then as one of the country's best milers against Mike Stahr from New York at both on Fifth Avenue and at the Millrose Games.

But on the last lap, in control of the race and staring at the first high school sub-10:00 run ever, Vance Watson of Willingboro started sliding up from behind. The roar rose up from the stands in a wave the way it only does at Penn and Carlo didn't hear his competitor approaching. By the time he saw the blue movement out of the corner of his right eye on the very short finishing straight, it was too late to respond. The two anchor men dove at the line and the clock captured them both in identical time.

From our perch in the east stands, it was too close to tell. The anxiety of the moment lingered. We waited. And waited. And waited, talking and trying to understand what we'd just seen. Sure, it was a Bernards victory. Sure Carlo got him in the lean. We stood shaking our heads.

Tick - tick- tick - tick. Then, the microphone clicked and an announcement.

When the call was made, more eyes saw Watson cross the line first. Willingboro in a dead heat victory. The next day, Vance Watson would be named high school athlete of the meet after he ran 1:53 to anchor his team to the 4 x 800m championship. A full eight seconds ahead of our Mounties' 7:48 in fifth place.

But it was a family thing that afternoon in the east stands. All of us cheering together. In triumph. In disappointment. In amazement.

So yes, it's the chest. Because it contains the heart. And sometimes it seems as if the heart might just break through and show itself to the world.

# Inside My Head

# 7

"Spoon feeding, in the long run, teaches us nothing
but the shape of the spoon."

- E.M.Forster

I never announced my retirement from competitive running.

Maybe I should have.

Told the world my story regardless of whether it wanted to hear it or not. Because when you don't, people presume they know already anyway.

It's like when we asked Aiden last night if he'd seen "Field of Dreams" and he said "yes" even though I was sure he'd never heard "if you build it, he will come" before in his life.

But that didn't stop him from telling us a long, detailed story of a movie that matched the title inside his head. I'd pay to see that movie.

And maybe that's why you need to announce your retirement even though no one wants it. We could each use our own little P.R. agency for ourselves.

It's like the radio. No one asked the DJ to play that song, she just guessed that based on what they played before, it was a song or a band you'd like. Maybe she guessed right. Maybe the DJ just played a song she liked hoping you'd be enthusiastic about it, too. But in the end, it's radio and not a playlist. So you can't skip ahead to the next best-guess song you already know you like. Or love. You just have to listen through. Even though you've never heard it before. Or heard it a thousand times in 1985—like Phil Collins' Sussudio. Or maybe you don't like it and need to listen through to the DJ's next best-guess for you. Aiden hates this. I'm afraid it's taught him impatience.

But he has a deep sense of curiosity about things so I don't worry much.

I never announced my retirement from professional running and racing. I was never a professional. Never had the chance. And I didn't really retire so much as the sport or my body retired me. Or the situation surrounding me at the time. The people making choices about me around me I couldn't control. I had no control over. Like a radio station I was listening to. WNEW New York and Carol Miller telling us to get the Led out in Zeptember.

The pain started almost right away that first fall season at Villanova. For training we'd run over to Harriton High School to run loops around their sports fields. 600m loops. 800m loops. Combine them in ways to make 1000m loops. Hard left turns. Square left turns. Always left turns. Always hard, square turns. I wasn't fit enough to run that fast that time of year. It was completely foreign from what I was used to. Old fashioned interval work translated to cross-country season. It confused me, but I was game. Listened to the instructions from Jenks and Pyrah—that's Villanova coaches Charles Jenkins and Jack Pyrah. What the heck—Pyrah had his fingerprints on a flurry of cross-country NCAA championship trophies. So who was I to question?

Jenks told me "25 miles a week" when I asked him what I should be doing to prepare over the summer. I should have known not to listen.

Known better. But I was going to his program. And he had a gold medal—so who was I to think for myself? I did more than he asked, but not as much as I should have. It was an odd summer for me anyway.

My mom took away my caddie job.

I'd been carrying golf bags at Somerset Hills Country Club every summer since I was, like, thirteen. Twelve and a half; the earliest I could get working papers. I had friends. And fun. And regular golfers who liked me. But my mom thought I wasn't working enough. Not making enough money. It wasn't a real job, she said.

She wanted me to have a "real job." Wanted me to want one. She had a friend who worked in the office at another Somerset Hills. Out on Mount Airy Road. Her friend told her they were looking for a groundskeeper that summer at Somerset Hills Memorial Park. So I went over to meet Andy, the 80-year-old man who ran the show.

It wasn't a summer job as it turned out. It was a career job. I didn't know this until I started working there. And my mom convinced me I wanted the job. So I didn't tell them anything about running or scholarships or my plan to start at Villanova at the end of August.

They hired me. And my new boss, Bryan, who was just standing in for the actual boss, Frank, who was home recovering from a motorcycle crash taught me how to run the mowers. And sharpen the blades on the grinding wheel. And how to double-clutch the old dump truck. And how to use the backhoe to dig a perfect rectangle in the soft earth not exactly 6-feet down, but about a foot deeper than the end of the shovel. And how to climb down into the hole with a spade to square the bottom and measure the depth over my head into a rectangular view of the blue, Garden State sky.

How to mix concrete and mortar to repair the inside of the crematory. And plant bronze plaques into the ground. A memorial park differs from a cemetery in that they don't have standing headstones. All the markers are flat to the ground making it easier to take care of the lawns.

We'd pick up lunch at Brush's Deli in Basking Ridge and talk working-guy talk. They were all from Ridge. Which didn't matter except we didn't really know the same circle of people. I learned more than I ever thought I'd know about cemeteries. But mostly, I'd say, I just cut grass.

And I did the training I was asked to do that summer. But it didn't prepare me for what I was supposed to be able to do on the trails of Bethlehem, Pennsylvania in October and November. And if I'm being honest, I knew it.

I've always had a happy talent for making things more difficult than they need to be. Probably comes from my mom. I was a graduate of the Agnes Smith School of Following the Rules. It didn't take long to realize I wasn't as fit as I wanted to be. I had so much muscle memory I could fake some of it, but you can't fake five miles at race pace.

I started trying to catch up. Knowing I had time because I was "really" there for track season. But cross was important. And fitness this time of year matters. But we were running long and short rectangles around these Main Line soccer fields. And it didn't make sense to me. And no one was explaining it to me no matter how much or often I asked. I heard the older guys, the Irishmen, Gerry O'Reilly and Sean O'Neill, trained with Tom Donnelly out at Haverford, but they never invited me. I don't know why. Maybe I wasn't Irish enough. It seemed to be an open secret that the top distance guys got their workouts from Donnelly instead of out of the Jake Nevin Field House.

Back home on Wednesday, we'd be banging it out on the trails of Jockey Hollow for 12 or 15 miles of hills and sweat and spit. And here, we were running repeat intervals all together. Is this how you prepare for a championship? And my feet were feeling weird. But that was probably just all the training trying to catch up on fitness. Or was it?

There was no Internet then. No email or social media. Mobile phones were only something you saw in limousines in movies and there was no such thing as text messaging. We didn't even have phones in our rooms. We had pay phones in the dorm hallway. We had a mailroom and brightly colored university stationery with designs. And stamps. And time waiting for hand-written letters to cross in the post. It was the only way to connect with our old friends who understood our experience and it wasn't helpful to my understanding of what I was experiencing.

Postmarks from New Jersey and Virginia and Tennessee kept connections from disappearing. Homesickness ebbed and flowed.

By winter, it would be worse.

# The Pump

# 8

*"As iron sharpens iron,
so one person sharpens another."*

- Proverbs 27:17

Winter in New Jersey can be rough. Not Buffalo rough. Not Minneapolis rough. But rough. Heather says it turns gray in November and the sun doesn't come out again until April. The truth is, it's not as bad as all that most of the time, but it can be cold, snowy, rainy, often raw and windy. That kind of Irish cold that you feel in your bones if you're not dressed for it. Even if you are dressed for it. But some days, it can swing the other way. Fifty-plus degrees can feel warm with a little sun breaking through the clouds into a clear blue sky.

That's how this one winter afternoon in 1985 began.

I honestly don't remember where everyone else was. Jeff Simpson may have been prepping for the World Junior Cross-Country qualifier. But Mark sent Pete Beckwith and me out for a twelve miler. Out six, back six. The Pump Course that we didn't run very often at all. We usually only did out five back five for ten on the 20 course. But he wanted us to run negative splits for the run. Six miles tempo on the way back in.

In the summer, the out 5 course was beloved. Steve Bailey's grandmother lived on Cherry Lane in Mendham. Just a half mile down from the turnaround—and she had a pool! We'd run out there in the heat, ten or twelve or more of us. A quick five and a half for a swim.

We'd swim and throw a nerf football around. Sun ourselves. Rest for a few minutes in the shade. Until our nylon shorts dried—smelling of chlorine. Swimming pools were not a usual thing in the Somerset Hills in those days.

And then a drag of five and a half back to the school in the paved humidity. Up and over Hardscrabble Road. It was the first five miles of the 20 course. And running it as part of another, shorter run made the first part of our Sunday long runs feel a little easier for me. A little more achievable. I still wish I was a more enthusiastic 20-miler like so many of my old cohorts.

But this day was just Pete and me. Maybe 48 or 50 degrees when we started. Shorts and long sleeves. Six miles out along the 20 course. Chatting about God knows what 16-year-olds thought was important on any given weekday. Pete and I were friends for a long time. Running together since we were what, 9 or 10 years old? We knew and loved each others' parents. Hung at each others' houses. Pete's family lived just up from the high school on Highview Avenue. Next-door neighbors to the Meyers who also figure into the Long Red Line. Amy ran at the highest High School level, was a state champion and ran on the 1983 Penn Relays Championship of America 4 x 800 team. Her little sister Jenny was in Pete's and my class, was a national class swimmer who ran with us, too. I remember their dad, Bob, running up and over Stevens Street past my house almost every spring and summer evening. Shorts, shirtless, fit and fast with the sun going down.

There was still a little snow melting under the canopy of the woods, but the roads were mostly dry. Childsworth and Old Colony.

Across the intersection onto Childs Road and eventually a left onto Hardscrabble just before the Old Mill and Route 202.

Pete and I were very close as youngsters but went slightly different ways as we got into junior high then high school. We always ran together. But we were closer then. His older brother, Tom, ran with us through the Junior Olympic days. So many of our tribe had siblings running. I had Emily, but she was into her own thing and I never had a brother, so these guys were the closest humans I ever had in my life.

This run was the most one-on-one time Pete and I spent together in a few years. It felt good and I felt strong on the road. Confident in my assignment. Six out steady. Easy. Then take it up tempo 6:15 a mile or faster on the way back home. Negative split it. Let Pete hang as long as he can. He was sixth or seventh man. I was first or second man all cross-country although Jeff had a solid grip on the first slot come championship season. I was anchor man coming into track season so the expectation was that I would lead Pete out on this one.

Roll up the little hill just before the trail head to Flatrock at Old Army Road then past Tim Scherman's family's place and the lake at Chestnut. Up and over the rise to Mount Kenya, then Jockey Hollow Road where Pete Carroll's parents lived.

The sky was graying and it was all cool air. We were dressed right. Warm and no gloves required. Lean and fast 16-year-olds. Pete may have already been 17. I wouldn't get there until May. Bernards Invitational week.

We pushed each other a little but not too much. Still a ways to go to the turnaround and not time to turn down the screws yet. I could drop him later.

Up the steady annoying climb past Washington Corner Road then past the horse farms—the only flat part on Hardscrabble. Down the steep, long, straightaway to Cherry Lane and the five-mile mark.

We turned left away from Steve Bailey's grandmom's house and up the steep hill to #6. No swimming this time of year. Just serious work to come.

We looked for the little pump house over the top of the hill that marks the turnaround—rolling over the whoop-dee-doos at the high point of Mendham. Then we turned for home and I picked up the pace. Pete started lagging and I was sure I was hitting the assignment glancing my wrist for time every so often. Rolling down the hill back to Hardscrabble. I knew I was about 6:00-6:15/mile with Pete fading in behind me. I climbed the long straightaway hill in reverse feeling the effort in my chest then, taking a peek behind for my buddy. There he was. Maybe 100m back. "Good for him," I said in my arrogant internal voice. I picked it up as I descended the winding part back down to Jockey Hollow Road and the entrance to Mount Kilimanjaro, the trail hill we ran over and over again. I peeked and not only was Pete still there, he was gaining. "That's not right," I thought. "need to knock this out now."

I started pushing for real. I was supposed to have him out of range by now. But he was still hanging on. By Flatrock, he was within 50m. I pushed up and over the little rollers and made the right back onto Childs where I'd be able to see down the lengthy straightaway. A gentle, almost but not completely flat incline back to the school. Pete was still there and gaining—I just couldn't drop the son of a gun. We climbed Childs, then Old Colony—the most irritating and last part of the run. Left on Childsworth and past the phone pole at the corner of the school property to beep my Casio to stop time. So much faster, the second half. Mission accomplished just a couple of steps ahead of Peter.

Never underestimate anyone on any day. Especially the ones you train with every day. Because they're doing the same work, or the same kind of work. They are capable of just about anything you are on any given run.

5:34/mile for the last six miles. 33:24.

That was a 10k PR for me on the second half of a 12 mile run. Just one training run at 16 years old that I remember to this day.

# WORKOUT: Master Blaster 1

### OCTOBER 1982, MONDAY

Mark introduced a new workout on the Polo Grounds course one day. He called it the Master Blaster. We were to do repeat start sections of he course at race pace. Measured out at about 400m. More like 450, really. But it was across grass and up a rise and down through a swale where two seasons before, we all helped Tim Peters put in wooden rails and wood chips to renovate the course as his Eagle Scout project. It was Mark's invention, but as usual, Mr. Mather loved the name and he repeated it often. "Mater Blaster! Who's the Master Blaster?"

It was repeat quarters, basically. But on a cross-country surface. Racing shoes. Race pace as a group, so we were keeping up with Carlotti and Blanchet and the other top guys. We were to take turns at the lead. Then the same leader to jog around the rest of the field, about another 350m, that was the interval.

We were all to keep up with the leader, then start the next repeat on a rolling start. If you dropped off the back before the start of the next, you were out. We were to do as many as we could until there was only one guy, the Master Blaster, left.

The time almost didn't matter. We all knew what race pace meant. And we all made it through the first four, looking around to see how everybody else was feeling. I started thinking of them in pairs. Two more, then two more. Just hang on. Mark pulled me and a couple of others out after ten. Carlo and Blanchet were still going head to head after 14. I think Mark called it a draw after one more.

Then we went for a four miler warm-down back to the school and home for dinner and homework and sleep before tomorrow. I think we had a dual meet on Wednesday.

There were many workouts we did over and over again in those days. Not usually every week, but maybe every two. Sometimes every three. Mark's schedule was consistent, but never completely predictable.

Some workouts only came up every so often. Some changed radically, out of necessity over time. Like Omni (more on that tragicomedy of a workout later). Just know for now, the first time we tried Omni is still a life trauma for many of us.

The Master Blaster was more of a legend. A story. Something we warned each other about. I only remember doing it truly twice. The first was that day at the Polo Grounds when Carlotti and Blanchet went nose-to-nose.

The other still sticks in my head today, 38 years later.

# Pixie Dust

## 9

"You tear apart the baby's rattle and see what makes the noise inside, but there is a veil covering the unseen world which not the strongest man, or even the united strength of all the strongest men that ever lived, could tear apart."

- Francis Pharcellus Church,
Yes, Virginia. There is a Santa Claus.

In an appearance on Stephen Colbert's show to promote his autobiography, Bruce Springsteen talked about "the magic trick."

"Before you go in there, it's an empty space, an empty building... and the audience is gonna come and you're gonna show up and together, you're going to manifest something that's very, very real," he described. "It's very tangible. But you're going to pull it out of thin air. It wasn't there before you showed up. It didn't exist. It's real magic."

And if you've ever been to a Springsteen show, or any other truly great live performance, you'll understand what that means.

He described it as "if you could have your first kiss on a nightly basis..."

Real magic, indeed.

←← →→

Human beings have a need to believe in magic and as much as I have a personal need to ask questions and understand the noise inside the baby's rattle, I need magic, too. I read a book once called "Will in the World," about the historical character William Shakespeare. It was an exploration built on the idea that the guy we know as Will Shakespeare couldn't possibly—with his "middle class" upbringing and education—have written the 38 plays and 154 sonnets we know today from William Shakespeare, the legendary poet and playwright.

It is an excellent book by Stephen Greenblatt I picked up in the British Library Shop.

My curiosity loved the book, but my humanity hated the idea. There is so little magic left in the modern world and I really love the idea that a regular kid from Stratford, 100 miles and a million ideas from the cultural center of the time, created the single best catalog of stories and observation of the age and our human condition.

In a note of geographical harmony, I'll point out here that Franklin Field is about that same 100-mile distance from the Bernardsville Square as Stratford to London.

So when Jonathan Gault of LetsRun.com called me out of the blue one day for an article he was working on about "the Wetmore formula," I had to chuckle to myself a little bit.

I told him I'd have to ask Mark first, but sure, I'd be happy to give him my opinions. Mark, of course, didn't care. "Tell him anything," he said to me.

So when I got back on the phone with Gault, and he started dancing around the question he really wanted to ask, I stopped him in his tracks.

"If you'd like, we can just cut to the chase," I said.

"What do you mean?"

"I could just give you the answer you're looking for if you want."

"What am I looking for?"

"I could tell you what the Wetmore Factor is. But you're going to be disappointed."

[Pause]

"Ok. Tell me."

"Number one. Show up on time. And two. Do the work."

[Pause]

"You're right. I'm disappointed."

I don't remember everything else we talked about. You can look up the article on LetsRun.com. I remember it being pretty good. It's under "The Wetmore Formula." And lots more has happened in track & cross-country and at the University of Colorado since then, but it holds up as at least an historical record of a moment in time.

We talked for at least an hour. And I've talked about this with many of my old running friends over the years. How there was no magic. No pixie dust. They all want pixie dust. A secret. A Houdini-esque mystique to it all. And there isn't really. If you saw the work those guys did over the summer. Hallinan. Logan. Carlotti. Nielsen. All the other guys who weren't first man on the team but ran extraordinary workouts every, single, day. The magic is in the effort. And you see it in other sports, too.

There was a reason the golfing great Ben Hogan was called "Mr. Hogan" by everyone but his very few closest friends. He was a serious fellow. When they asked him what the secret to his swing was, he said "you dig it out of the dirt." And it's the same here.

[Pause]

But maybe.

If I'm being honest, there's a little more to it than that.

How did Wetmore, this unique, reputationally anti-social, intellectual, forever polite man get this batch of youngsters—teenagers no less—to WANT to show up and work so hard every single day? Because there weren't really any days off. Sure there were rest days. Very important to rest. And travel days and "active rest" between seasons. But there were really no days off. You can look at any of our log books from those days and see that.

And we all turned up ready to run.

And we all knew the stories.

Buck Logan's state two-mile record. John Sullivan's three-flat at Penn. Buck and John were our friends, sure, but they graduated seven years ahead of me. That's a lifetime in high school years. They were also my heroes.

Ed Mather built a tradition on a feeling of running away from home to join the circus. It never felt like a school team with him. It felt like something outside of all that. A commitment to something bigger. He had an almost mystical ability to get young people to follow him out to the cross country course. He made them all feel as if they'd been tapped, selected, genetically gifted to be part of a secret society that everyone else wanted to know about.

Even though he came up through that same program, Mark Wetmore's approach was different. More serious to match his personality. He had a way of talking to us that made everything feel important. Achievable and businesslike, but important. Like there was a pathway to something excellent if you had the heart to believe in yourself. If you were able to throw off fear and show your mettle. A way to success that could be yours if only you had the nerve to commit to it.

In 1983, he put it down on paper. Type-written on his old manual typewriter, he ran off mimeographed duplicates to hand out. He branded the summer training program he'd been running for years. A program that simply did not exist anywhere else.

"Attention Serious Runners," it began. "The Mine Mountain Road Department in conjunction with Sysyphus Synergetics Syndicated presents: *CAMP PAIN*"

For those of us with some experience and understanding of the method, he captured our attention. For those new to the program, this ignited their imagination. Two pages explained it all in clear, simple, terms. The basic plans that only required a financial cost. The "Black Plan" discounted for MMRD members and the "Green Plan" for non-MMRD members. Then, the "White Plan" available at a cost of "strict adherence."

Camp Pain Secret Dossier #SU83013

WHITE PLAN
There has been an expression of interest in the Camp Pain White Plan. Space does not permit an in-depth examination of this plan, but following is a brief explication.

My coaching services are available for free to those who agree with and are willing to adhere to the following principles of conduct:

Time - You will be at practice punctually every day forever. You will leave when you have been excused. You will observe an 11:00 curfew every night but Friday. Friday night is to be concluded by midnight. You will never sleep beyond 9:00 a.m. Sleeping late is for infants, anarchists, and house plants.

Citizenship - The sword of expectation hangs over your head. Your conduct is an expression of our respect for your family, community, faith, and yourself. You will regularly (I will check) volunteer for work at home for free.

Study - The sole function of childhood is learning. The quality of your adult life will be effected by nothing as significantly as by your education. If our relationship lasts into the school year, your G.P.A. will go up every marking period, or you will no longer exist.

Diet - You will eat intelligently three times per day. Candy and soda are for weaklings who have failed to install more substantial gratifications in their lives.

Intoxicants. Alcohol and drugs are destructive physically, emotionally, and spiritually. The idea that there is any space, however small, in the life of an athlete for intoxicants is absurd and ridiculous. Television is similarly dangerous. Television viewing is allowable only with parental supervision.

Romance - I do not believe in adolescent romance, but I accept that this is widely divergent from most popular opinion. Therefore the degree to which you pursue and participate in romance is the responsibility of your parents, but the degree to which I must be involved in these romances is up to me. I don't want to hear about it, witness it, or see it effect your work with me. No longing gazes, no whispered spats, no surreptitious hand holding. I have never known a high school athlete that survived a childhood romance.

Remember, participation in the White Plan is voluntary. Other plans are available at a much more affordable cost. Think carefully before undertaking such an extreme method.

Having these secret communications in hand felt like a unique opportunity, even for those of us already bought-in to the program. Both entertaining and motivating, it identified those individuals willing to commit. And it worked.

Aiden doesn't like it when I say I'm old. I'll sometimes say I'm an old, slow, fat man when I'm trying to keep up with him.

I get it. And I'm probably a lot tougher on myself than I ought to be, but it feels true when I'm out there plodding the slow steps of a former runner and breathing heavy. But then, once in awhile, and regrettably when I'm alone, I have one of those runs that feels just fantastic and I start that unhealthy thinking like I'm 17 again and start pushing harder than I ought to. And hopefully I'll remember I'm 56 before something breaks down.

I took Aiden to the last Pac-12 track championship at Potts Field in Boulder in May. I didn't know what to expect of my first meet since moving there a few months before. I reached out to Mark to see if we could catch up. He was busy with the details, of course, but when I told him we were coming, he wrote back, "Good. Buck Logan and John Sullivan should be somewhere."

The more often I hear from Mark, the more impressed I am with his economy of language and his ability to communicate so much in such a small amount of ink.

Frankly, I'm jealous. I don't think it's an accident that when he was quoting Hemingway to us, I was more interested in Fitzgerald.

But it had to be almost 20 years since I'd seen Buck or John in person. Maybe a little less for John. I'm sure I'd seen him at a Pie Run on one Thanksgiving Day or another up at the Polo Grounds. And I wondered if any of us would recognize each other.

It was Aiden's first big meet as a spectator. I was introducing him to the sport I loved the way my dad did with me at an IC4A meet at Jadwin when I was a little younger than him. Answering questions. Trying not to miss anything and looking for John and Buck in the crowded seats.

It took several trips up and down the aisles of the metal grandstand, but eventually, I spotted someone I thought was Buck. Same slim build. Same serious face. A bit grayer, but more hair than I have left.

"Buck!" I called out approaching through the crowd.

I don't think he recognized me at first, but it only took a moment and an intro to Aiden to start the next three hours of conversation, observation, and running commentary on the meet we were watching—and the old days.

It's funny what happens when you run into someone you spent a lot of time with a long time ago. In almost no time, you fall into familiar patterns. Talking. Connecting as if you saw each other just yesterday.

Turns out, we missed John by just a few minutes. He'd come out to see his daughter compete and rushed off to catch a flight home. Honestly, I didn't know either of these guys the way they knew each other, but we'd all chewed up so much of the same turf over the years, we felt like family. At least that's how it felt to me.

I'm not sure what Aiden thought. He said it was a little overwhelming for him, but he absolutely loved it.

Buck was excited about heading out to Eugene for the US Olympic Trials where he'd spend time with Hallinan, Stogryn, Pete Carroll, and

Brad Hudson. Gault called Buck and a few of the other old guard for his article. We all told him some version of the same story so we talked about that. And three hours later...

I live nearby now, but these guys traveled hundreds of miles. John from Bernardsville where his sister, Megan, lives in their childhood home. Buck from Washington, D.C. Each to see a track meet and cheer on the college kids we didn't know coached by a man who meant so much to us. Who we'd barely see during the trip. But it was important for us all to be there. Especially this year, we'd find out later.

I think Aiden felt it, too. Even without the history, he became part of it all.

So I got to hang out with Buck. And just missed John. I don't know what they would think if they heard me call them my heroes. And Peter Carroll and Chris Hallinan. And closer, Blanchet, Stogryn, Carlotti. Friends, but heroes? All of them. And legendary stories I thought about every summer day we trained together. Mark talking about his friends in high school. Some were coaches and teachers like Joe Laspada and Dave Sully. Some came around with their own kids later like Tom Lewis and Brian Bomberger and Ed Johnson. Some just phantoms we'd never meet from stories we'd heard so many times before like Jamie Blair.

Floating up Olcott Avenue to Old Army Road headed to Flatrock.

Smelling the new oil and tar and gravel on Mendham Road on our way out to the big hill on Bliss.

Feeling the cool morning mist on our shoulders as we started out on the 20 course every Sunday all together until we hit the first hill on Hardscrabble and started to pay attention to the task at hand.

Dripping puddles of sweat earned with a five mile tempo run in the middle of a 10 mile push through the swamp—The Great Swamp National Wildlife Refuge in Basking Ridge for those not familiar.

We'd all come in one at a time drenched from the 90ish degree temperatures and 80+ percent humidity of the New Jersey summer. We'd camp out on the wall in front of Bernards High School all together asking about all sorts of things from the run to the music to the girls or the girls about the boys or intentionally not about the boys. Only sometimes about the meets to come. Guzzling cold water melted from frozen old plastic milk jugs trying to rehydrate in a day where you didn't use the word "rehydrate." Mark giving us inspiration from Hemingway or Dostoevsky or Tom Wolfe. Larry Sullivan explaining strength and speed to me by drawing two boxes in the dirt. How one can grow, but the other has a genetic max. We ran every day with our friends and our heroes. So if you're searching hard enough for magic, maybe that's it. Maybe that's the pixie dust. Maybe we manifested some real magic after all.

# Pain

# 10

> "I've stood here before inside the pouring rain
> With the world turning circles running 'round my brain
> I guess I'm always hoping that you'll end this reign
> But it's my destiny to be..."
>
> - Gordon Matthew Sumner

I woke up in pain. Again. I honestly don't remember a day when I didn't wake up in some level of pain. Not 10 out of 10 pain. But maybe 5 or 6 out of 10 pain.

A lot of times, things really are funny because they're true. I remember on Thanksgiving morning, probably about 2005. Cold. Damp. A little rainy. Certainly muddy. Pete Carroll got out of his car at the Pie Run and overheard someone saying something about the cold and feeling stiff and sore.

"I'm glad I'm a distance runner," he said. "I feel like this all the time."

So basically, nothing to complain about.

"This is the best I'm going to feel all day."

That idea registered right away and stuck with me.

I don't remember when I first felt the pain in my foot, but it was early on. That first fall at Villanova. I do remember when it started to get bad.

I'd been to the docs multiple times. Dr. English was one and his two partners in Bryn Mawr. They all sort of listened to my story and all told me the same thing— "it's just tendonitis. Give it some rest and keep training."

Several bottles of Motrin, a badly-fitted pair of $300 dollar orthotics and multiple appointments later, it was worse. But the advice hadn't changed.

Eventually, I couldn't walk across the street to get to my final exams. I turned back from the crosswalk at N. Gulph Road to climb the St. Mary's stairs back to my room. Nine months. Eleven months. Twelve or thirteen months of misdiagnosis. No help from the Villanova training room staff who were far more interested in the football and basketball players. Dan—something. Arrogant, bitter guy with a mustache. There's nothing worse than skinny mustachioed arrogance. It has the vibe of unearned entitlement and pedophilia.

No help from the coaches' office. I was clearly hurt and not getting any better. Never been hurt in my running career before. I asked about red-shirting the year but Jenks ignored me to my face. The head coach clearly did not want to be talking to me in his office. To be honest, I wasn't sure if he understood what I was asking or what red shirting was.

Red Shirting is an option for sports programs of the NCAA— where an athlete can sit out a varsity season to extend his or her eligibility a year. Designed to enable the new, younger athletes to still train, but not compete with their team, attend classes, receive academic tutoring, etc. and grow into the strength they need to compete at the collegiate level. It is also often used for athletes who are injured to be able to take the time to recover and heal without exhausting a full season of eligibility under the terms of their scholarship. Basically, they can be declared on the injured list for the season so you could have a student junior but a red-shirt sophomore. Athletes can and often do complete their fourth year of athletic eligibility during their first year of graduate study.

I talked to Jack Pyrah about it, too. With about the same result. Either no understanding or no interest. Maybe Villanova didn't use the Red Shirt rule in those days.

So here I am. Spring. Freshman. Hurt. Can't train. Heck, can't really walk. Doctors seemingly more interested in cashing checks from their Villanova University contract than taking care of their patient-athletes. The best they could do for me was fit me for a pair of orthotics that never fit properly and gave me crippling blisters on my arches. Then they all... the doctors, the trainers, the PTs, the coaches all complained about how much everything cost. The orthotics were "expensive orthotics." They didn't want to do a bone scan for a proper diagnosis because it was a "$400 bone scan." I was just a kid. With no one on my side. Who didn't realize he had an argument to make against all of this.

I rode the Villanova van to Bryn Mawr Orthopedic Associates to see them. Once or twice I saw one of them or another in the training room. Always, it was the same. As if they'd never seen me before. As if there was no memory of me as a returning patient—even with my chart—three doctors, three partners, each started with me from scratch every time. I wondered if they ever had trouble getting their comped basketball tickets from Will Call at the Spectrum.

Dan, the head trainer fawned over the docs like they were wearing tights, capes and a large letter G on their chests. The God-complex is a real thing under those white coats. I was lost in a blizzard of repetitive, bad advice. I wondered if anyone reported anything to the coaches. It seemed like no one knew anything. Nine, ten, twelve months or more of "It's just tendonitis. Keep training," making me feel like I'm weak or making up a story about it all until I couldn't put weight on my left foot hardly at all.

It was Mark, finally, who told me I should get an appointment with Dr. Leach in Boston.

Mark knew Dr. Robert Leach by reputation and experience. He was the surgeon who worked on Paul Stogryn's knee years before after he fell on the ice on Mine Mount Road in 1981 and tore his lateral collateral ligament. Paul missed most of the spring season his junior year wearing a hip-to-ankle cast and ended up coming back at the end of cross-country season to knock a promising freshman off the state championship team.

Paul went on to make the US Junior Cross-Country Team as a high schooler—rare to say the least—and ran in the 1983 World Junior Championship in my grandfather's home town of Gateshead in England.

Jenks and Pyrah knew I was going to see a specialist. Neither showed any particular interest in what might come of it. Neither recommended anyone in Philadelphia.

It was a typical, intensely hot Philadelphia late Fall day that smelled of new blacktop and cut grass the day I flew to Boston alone. Thirty-seven minutes in the air to Logan Airport aboard a People's Express jet and a subway ride—they called it the Metro—to Boston University Hospital. I was plenty early for my appointment with nothing to do and no one to see, so I limped around the sweaty summer sights. I saw the Bull & Finch from the outside—Cheers. Signs for the Patriots Path. I heard the Charles River was over that way, but the walk was too long for my foot.

Eventually, I found my way into Dr. Leach's waiting room, filled out the necessary forms and was ushered into a cramped exam room.

Dr. Leach was one of those famous sports-world surgeons. The Celtics. The Patriots. The Red Sox. If it could be fixed, he was the guy. He was the first person I felt listened to me at all. He listened to my story as if he actually cared, or at least as if he was trying to figure out the puzzle that was me. He was kind. And interested. A new medical experience for me.

He pointed and poked at the place on my bare foot where I said it hurt. He rotated my foot on its ankle and thought for a very short moment with a look that said he'd seen it before.

"Stress fracture," he said.

He said he believed it to be tarsal navicular, like Bill Walton, he said. "Career threatening," he said. To be sure, he ordered me to get a bone scan when I got back to Philly. Send him the results, he said. MRI wasn't a thing at that time.

I felt like I was losing everything in a city I hardly knew at all. The diagnosis I feared most. Part of me defeated, part of me itching to prove Leach wrong. I wished my dad was there with me. Before cell phones. No way to talk to anybody in the moment. Just something I suffered through on my own.

When I got back to Philly, riding the SEPTA train alone out to the Villanova station and limped my way back up to my dorm, that phrase, those words, "career threatening" were still vibrating through my mind.

Leach just shook his head as I told him my history with the doctors at Bryn Mawr. The Bryn Mawr "plan." He rolled his eyes. Didn't criticize.

They never do. They tend not to call each other on the carpet, doctors, their fields being as much art as science sometimes.

I just wanted to get back on my feet training. That's all. I never would. Not really.

Jenks sent me back to Dan, the mustachioed pedo trainer, and somebody referred me to another doc at Penn. So I had to go see another doctor just to get the bone scan ordered by Dr. Leach in Boston. Because "the bone scan is very expensive." So afraid they all were of the $400 they'd have to spend on the test.

When I met Dr. Torg at Penn, I expected to feel the same way I did in Bryn Mawr. His was a dreary, dark, dusty, poorly lit office in an old brick building. I couldn't tell if he did or didn't believe me. Either that or he thought I was a lost cause. A college runner, not a pro athlete. Or maybe he didn't like that I'd come from Dr. Leach in Boston. I learned later Torg was basically Leach's Philadelphia counterpart. The Sixers. The Eagles. The Phillies. Competition on reputation is tough to swallow. The Bryn Mawr docs treated me like I was trying to get away with something. Like I hadn't earned my way there with 100-mile weeks on the roads and trails of Bernardsville. With fast races and Championships of America and 16 individual state titles. They treated me like I was trying to steal their wallets from their top desk drawers while their backs were turned. ALL OF THEM. Same as Dan, the arrogant, angry trainer. Same as the coaches. And the team was starting to feel that same way. But I couldn't get a clear read on Dr. Torg. He was all business with me. No feeling. He told me the same story about the cost of a bone scan. I just wanted to find out if my career was over. I wanted to tell him I'd pay for the damned scan myself. I'd had enough of all of this. The Bryn Mawr country-club MDs talked me through a plan every time I talked to them. First, we'll try rest and ice, then, we'll try orthotics, then, we'll maybe do a bone scan, but that's very expensive *ping*, so that will be a last resort. I remember multiple people telling me $400 and thinking "THAT's what you think is expensive?"

The bone scan was finally scheduled and I had to take the SEPTA train back into Philly to get it done. They gave me some kind of radioactive something to drink, then placed me on a table where a big machine went back and forth over and over again scanning my foot. The bright green glow lit up the monitor like Christmas over the shadow of my foot on the little screen. That was the stress fracture. It was clear in just a few minutes that Dr. Leach was right out of the gate. The scan didn't even need to finish.

I visited Dr. Torg at Penn again to have him give me the same news Dr. Leach had already given me over the phone. Torg ordered me to be put in a cast for six weeks over finals and the Christmas holiday. Then, he said, it should be healed and I would need PT after that. Never a word about surgical options. Probably too expensive. I guess insurance doesn't mean anything in Philadelphia. Then he ushered me out of his dark office.

My first positive Philadelphia medical experience came a few days later, after Thanksgiving break, when I visited Dr. Gary Gordon at his Franklin Field office to get my cast put on. His office and training room overlooked the stadium, which made me feel both happy and nostalgic. He also was straight with me regarding the healing of my foot. Optimistic, but no magical thinking here. Again, no one anywhere along the journey to this point talked about surgery for me.

For more than six weeks, I wandered around Christmastime on crutches. I even went into New York to see Les Miserables with my sister on my crutches. The show was great. The traveling back and forth was awful. In the sleet. Eventually, I ended up back in Philly, riding the train on crutches to Franklin Field.

Dr. Gordon cut the cast off and started listing a series of exercises for me to get my left lower leg back to equal strength and flexibility to my right. He listened to me. He laughed easily. He made me feel like I was a real patient with a real journey to health to pursue. The walk back to 30th Street Station from Gordon's office that I thought would be light and easy without a cast and crutches, was long, and slow, and painful. Unused for six weeks, my left calf was screaming the entire way.

I traveled back and forth into the city on the train for PT, happy to escape Dan's training room. Again, as much as I liked Dr. Gordon, I couldn't understand the people who kept raising issue of cost who sent me back and forth to Penn every week. I paid for the travel expenses myself. Eventually, I was back in the training room and weight room at Villanova. As usual, I was on my own. No help. No direction. I asked. Made myself a pest in Jenks' office. But no marching orders ever came.

The first time I met Charles Jenkins was at the Manhattan Invitational at Van Cortlandt Park. I was a junior. Running well and being recruited by college all over the place. I'd talked to Jack Pyrah, his legendary assistant coach, on the phone a few times. My outsized sense of nostalgia had me picturing my life and success at 'Nova and, as usual, I couldn't wait to get ahead of myself.

I saw the two coaches on the field near the Broadway side. Pyrah was talking to friend and Villanovan Pete Carroll. I screwed up my courage to hopefully wangle an introduction. Forever helpful to me, Pete walked me over.

"Dr. Jenkins, this is Lyle Smith."

"Hi. Yes. Hello. Charles Jenkins," the tall former Olympian said to me almost whispering. Eyes wandering the horizon betraying his lack of interest in being at a cross-country meet or talking to someone like me.

I should have taken that as a big, blinking, red signal, but I was a kid. And he was one of the great Villanova Olympians. And that casts a haze on everything. And Jack Pyrah was there connecting me to the legendary Jumbo Elliot days. And I liked Jack Pyrah. Everybody liked Jack Pyrah. And I understood the friction of the Mather/Wetmore dynamic at work here. To have a head coach more interested in the public face and an assistant in charge of the underlying work of training. That made sense to me. So I figured it would be ok. I was used to it.

But years later, I can tell you every single time I saw or shook hands with Dr. Charlie Jenkins, it was the same.

"Hi. Yes. Hello. Charles Jenkins," as if we'd never crossed paths before.

And his eyes darted the horizon or the rest of the room searching for whatever might be more important than the conversation with which he was currently shaking hands.

He was a nice man. A kind man in many ways. I don't think he really meant it to be as remarkably rude and dismissive as it felt. But it was the same. Every time. He wasn't a coach. Not in the Jumbo, Wooden, Lydiard, Donelley, Wetmore kind of way. And they were all completely different from each other. And he never should have been put in charge of the development, health, and well-being of teams of young people. Ever.

It was Uncle Marty Stern, the women's coach and sneaker store entrepreneur who listened to me and got me running in a float vest in the pool. I liked Marty Stern. It was impossible not to like Marty Stern. Then it was John Marshall, Olympian, graduate of Villanova, 800m specialist from

Plainfield, New Jersey who guided me through some recovery workouts in the weight room and on the stationary bike. I was overwhelmed by John Marshall. He was larger than life to me. Olympian. A hero. Plus, he treated me as a friend. A kind of little brother from Jersey. Like Pete Carroll. Like Chris Hallinan. He made what he was seem achievable.

No help from Jenks or Pyrah. At all. I should have learned how to be a squeaky wheel by this time and demand it. Attention must be paid. But it just wasn't in my nature.

Let's put pin in this story here. We'll revisit what happens next in about 2006.

This is a story I kept to myself over the years. Never told anyone, really. I told Heather some of it, but I don't think I ever communicated how much it meant to me. It's embarrassing. It feels like losing when something that meaningful gets taken away. It feels like failure and you don't want to share that with anyone for risk of feeling judged.

That said, let's not have any confusion, either. This wasn't a cancer diagnosis. Nothing life-threatening here. No St. Jude's stories. Just a kid who couldn't run anymore. But maybe that was a part of the problem. The perception. How serious could it be, really? The perception that this should have been solved already. The perception that the only explanation for why it's taking so long is he must be trying to get away with something. Something for nothing.

I was so ashamed I only told my dad parts of it. Humiliated. Defeated. I always thought I might write it one day, but it wasn't until now that I could. Now that my own son is starting to run as a young freshman at Niwot High School.

What was my experience, really? Abuse? Neglect? Disinterest? It was a different time. But some ways exactly the same. My wife, the medical professional says this is PTSD.

The percentage of high school athletes who go on to play any sport professionally is .023 percent. That percentage among college athletes skyrockets to less than two percent. So to criticize a high school program for not turning out more Olympians is monumentally stupid.

Now set aside the data for a moment and ask, is it a matter of desire, because if it was, there are so many athletes I know personally who would have worn the red, white, and blue. Desire is only part of it. Talent, ability is only part of it. Dedication and resources are only parts of it. Pure, dumb luck is a part of it, too. And anyone who says different has only experienced the spectator side of it.

The knock on Mark Wetmore and the Bernards runners was that we were overtrained, injured, and burned out by the time we got to the college programs. I can't speak for the other guys and girls, but I never found any of that to be true. Not for me. I couldn't wait to get back to training. I couldn't wait to test myself against the other runners around me. I took every opportunity to talk to them at meets whether I was entered or not. Moreso when I wasn't running. I chased down John Trautmann at the Jumbo Elliott meet and gabbed with him along the fence line because I couldn't line up against him. Talking would have to do. I wasn't burned out. I was injured and discarded and tossed in the bin.

The Bernards burnout stories were no more true than the recruiting rumors about Bernards and Mr. Mather cheating the system. Another fable, provably false, that wouldn't die. Heck, I've been accused of being illegally recruited to Bernards. Not long ago. Years after I should have been forgotten to NJ track history. My family moved into town when I was four years old. If I was recruited in at that age, Ed Mather was even more magical than everybody already thought.

People believe what they want to believe. Heather says it the best way, I think. It's the people who believe everyone is out to steal from them who are most likely to be thieves. It's the people who are so sure everyone is lying to them who are most likely to be the best liars. And here, I'm one hundred percent sure it's those people who call you burned out or lazy or unmotivated who are the ones trying to get away with something. There is no free lunch. You have to fight to earn every bite. Everything that's important to you. Especially your physical and mental health.

# WORKOUT: Omni

Short morning was the first course I knew by name. I struggled to keep up with Mrs. Knox, Tasha and Rick's mom who ran with and looked after us youngsters. Tasha and Rick and Pete, Tom, and Tracey Hinman all ran ahead of me that first afternoon. Claremont to Mendham up Chestnut—a big hill my first time out. Up and over Old Fort to Olcott down to the High School again. Three miles we used to call it. Just less than, actually. Just about spot-on when you add the pool loop.

Years later, that was the first and last part of Omni. What became Omni, actually. The original Omni was much less running and far more traumatic.

It was 1982. A lot of experimental workouts happened in 1982. We all did a short warm-up and gathered together on the track. Boys and girls, both. It was winter—early in the season. And the perfect time for trying out new things. We'd done a very hard, but fun handicapped time trial a couple of weeks before in the wind. 1,500m and Mark had us all timed out by the second. Carlotti started behind me by something like 25 or 30 seconds. 28, I think. And it was my job to hold him off. Him and Blanchet and Jim Nielsen and to catch everybody else. Run with Mike Hinman and Mike Flood. To battle through the wind and try and figure out what I—we might be able to do come spring.

But Omni sounded ominous. None of us had any idea what it was or what to expect. These were the days of magazine profiles on Sebastian Coe and his coach/father and isometric exercises. Words we didn't yet understand very well. Plyometrics. Claims of world records run on 25 miles a week—phantom ideas built on the incomplete story we didn't know.

That only miles run at race pace counted—which meant closer to 100 miles a week, which made more sense—didn't make it into the profile.

So this was an introduction to a new type of training for us.

We all lined up as Mark demonstrated each exercise. Squat walks first. Step out into a squat, sort of a runner-inspired warrior pose. then step through as if running in a squat position. We all reached out farther than we ought to have done—deeper to the ground because it didn't feel like much compared to our miles and hill workouts. So we pushed on this gray, cold, wintery, New Jersey day. 100m of squat walks. Then run the rest of the lap.

Then springing. We were all familiar with this from doing our Lydiard springing up Rolling Hill Road—12 times—more? The assignments always changed—forever evolving. Springing down the track knees up high, vertically as high as we could get on each step. No skipping. Alternate feet like running in place. Not too fast down the track at once. Not about speed, all about height. Strength. Run a lap.

Then high knees. Really like running in place, this one. High—high—high. Knees up. Thighs parallel to the ground. 100m. Run the rest of the lap.

The soreness at the top-inside of our thighs starting to ache. All of us felt it. Is this what it's supposed to feel like?

Buzzers next. Run-sort-of. Pick up your feet just off the ground and back again. Left—right as fast as you can go. Moving forward as slowly as possible. Just fast. Fast. Fast twitch. 10 seconds x 3. Run the rest of the lap.

Frog hops. Squat down then explode forward as far as you can. Over and over for 50m. Then finish the lap.

Carioca next. Crossover legs left - right - left - right. 50 meters facing each direction. Finish the lap.

Then squat-thrusts. What we'd later call burpees. Springing straight up into the air hands to the clouds on each one. Twenty of them. Then finish the lap.

Then overstriding. Make each step 2-6 inches longer than usual as you run down the straightaway. If it doesn't feel weird, you're not doing anything different. Not a sprint, but fast. It has to be a little fast just to get your stride out that far. 100m. Then finish the lap.

Legs feeling it front and back of both thighs but really, really the high-inside crotch spot from the squat walks. Painful, but that's what it was supposed to be, no?

Next set.

We all stayed. The whole of the first-ever Omni workout. Carlotti. Meg Waldron. Jenny Rahn. Steve Bailey. Jenny and Amy Meyer. All of us. There must have been 25 of us or more out there doing this oddball calisthenics-inspired workout wondering what the world was thinking of us from whatever far off view they had from their car windows.

It was all too much. That's what we learned that day. The squat walks especially. 200m of squat walks and none of us could walk for a week. We all had something new to commiserate about and that was when we learned—workouts are not immutable.

They needed to change based on a batch of specifics. Individual needs. Intensity. Time of year. Misjudged bullseye. On paper, it seemed perfect. In practice, it was waaaaay too much—especially for a first. It was a good thing none of us had to race any time soon. We wouldn't have been able to bend down to tie our spikes.

By fall of 1983, Omni had changed from an exercise in plyometric torture to a tough, fair workout most of us actually liked. Loved, even. I'm not sure Ranjan enjoyed it much, but he wasn't there for the first one. He didn't join us from Naperville until late spring of freshman year. Jim and Jeff and Stephen and Thomas Praisner and Jeff Friedman—all of us. Together.

With a new twist. Basically four parts. After a summer of base-training done and booked, reviewers and critics of Lydiard called it LSD — long slow distance. Mark told me that Lydiard would not like being credited for this concept. "Arthur would say, 'slow training leads to slow racing,'" he told me.

So Mark adjusted and adapted to necessities as he always did. In Bernardsville it was adapting to the needs of the young people. Later, in Boulder, it was adapting to the demands of three college seasons per year and altitude. It became "long fast distance." If you could maintain a comfortable conversation, he said, you weren't going hard enough.

Hot, muggy summer started to turn to cooler in the a.m. cloudier in the evening Autumn. We'd started a new thing we called a two-mile push.

Start the watch. Run 8 laps on feel. Fast. Feeling good. Banned from looking at the watch. We'd tape over the face so we couldn't cheat on splits. Pure feel.

The first ones were about 12 minutes. Over time, we started hitting closer to 10:00. Nielsen was running 9:30 or better on his 6 a.m. morning runs. It was hard. Hurt a bit. But built such confidence knowing nobody else was doing anything quite like it.

Then one dry, cool Tuesday afternoon, the new Omni!

The 200m of squat walks had been adjusted to sets of 15-20m, but this was something entirely new.

Look at the time so you could tell the full duration of the workout. Start at 3:30 on the dot-ish. Finish at 4:28 on the dot. That's 58 minutes total.

The assignment—short morning. The full short-morning down Seney Drive, around the pool road, then down Seney Drive again. Make it 3 miles. Then right to the track. 8 laps. Two-mile push from the 300m mark nearest the gate. Start the stopwatch and stop it at 8 laps—no peeking. Just feel. Tempo—eventually working it up to race pace-ish. Then 8 laps of Omni. Squat walks. Springing. High knees. Buzzers. Frog hops for the hips. 20m each. Then a quick rest of the lap. 20 burpees, then a lap. Carioca, then the rest of the lap. One to go. Anybody can do the last one. Over-striding 100m then carry yourself over one last lap. Look around at everybody else as you head back out on the road for a full Short Morning. The other way around this time. Up Seney Drive and around the pool loop. Then up Seney Drive again to Chestnut, Mendham, down Claremont in front of the massive glass window at Jeroloman's Store and back up to the High School. Finish at the crest of the speed bump.

Now—you can look at the watch.

4:24 p.m. :56 minutes. Just under ten miles. Time to stretch in that reluctant, painful, distance runner style.

All of us—everyone poised for varsity—8 or so. 9 or so. Boys side. Girls side. No more for such a small school. All of us would have to be ready in November to have a shot at All-Groups. A real shot. Seven healthy, nearly healthy ready to run. Hard. Focused. Wanting it. Wanting—needing to hold each other up. All friends connected by effort in ways we couldn't really explain to other people.

Just a typical Tuesday in September.

# THE COURSES

The courses all had names. We didn't all know where they all came from, but most were named for the roads in an old Gilded Age town.
- Pfizer-Ballantine
- Bliss
- Lloyd
- Pill Hill
- Boulderwood Loop
- Meeker
- Hub Hollow

Some were named for the places and houses and people who belonged to those places.
- Tap
- Jackie-O. Yes, THAT Jackie-O.
- Ridge
- Twin Lakes
- Jockey Hollow
- Gill Loop

Others just names that came from something else.
- Short Morning was the short morning run course.
- Long Morning was it's longer cousin.
- Flatrock was basically all the trail runs that went through the clearing where there was a big, flat rock and swimming hole.

- Named for the famed African mountains that inspired our hill workouts

Mt. Kenya, short-ish and steep; and

Mt. Kilamanjaro, long and steady.

- The Swamp was a 10-mile loop through Ridge and the Great Swamp National Wildlife Refuge. Gravelly and completely flat, as that name would have you understand.
- We ran hills in the woods in the snow once behind Wetmore's house. No trails. Just snow. No name. It was horrible.
- The Golf Course was the perimeter of Somerset Hills Country Club where they let us run most Mondays in the fall.
- The Course - was what I remember Mike Flood calling our home cross-country course at The Polo Grounds
- Hairpin Trail was the trail that ran out from the Polo Grounds to the hairpin turn on Old Army Road.
- Fun Run was the three-mile loop tied to the Bernards Half Marathon day.
- Runathon Loop was a one-mile loop near the high school we used for a fundraising run-a-thon one year. And for short warm-ups and extra miles every other day since.
- Morning circuit was the route we took past everyone's house in town to pick them up and dump them off three or more mornings a week. About 4 miles.
- Out 5, Back 5 was the first five of the 20-course and back.
- The Pump was the first six miles of the 20-course and back. The turnaround was a little old pump house at the top of the hill.
- The 20-Course. No additional explanation necessary.

And we ran from different home bases at different times in our history. The Wall. The Polo Grounds. The Flood's House. The Rec/Little League Clubhouse, Mark's house. In-season, when school was in session, but out for a holiday and not allowed to have "official practice," Mark would be sure to tell us the day before, "Whatever you do tomorrow, be sure you don't do… [description of workout here]." But in the end, we all knew where to be when we needed to be there together.

## Ultimate Afternoon

# 11

"There are two ways of spreading light:
to be the candle or the mirror that reflects it."

- Edith Wharton

The heavy, blue disc sailed across the field high and far into my hands just past the imaginary line made by two crumpled up t-shirts. Caught and landed and score! Another point for our side. Then Blanchet picked up the bee and threw it the other way to pass and catch and pass and catch their way to the road side of the field and score on that end. Back and forth. Scoring almost every time, but not every time. Turnovers when the disc got dropped. Laughing and running and pushing just enough to be interesting.

Ultimate Frisbee, sometimes called Frisbee football is a game developed by film producer Joel Silver and his buddies in the late 1960s. Another Jersey kid from Maplewood, Silver created the game inspired in part by soccer and American football but basically non-contact and self-officiating and steeped in the joy of caching and throwing. One of the other creators, Jared Kass, described the name coming from the feeling of catching a pass as "the ultimate game."

Silver had a success producing films from 48-hours and Brewsters Millions to the Lethal Weapon franchise and Commando and the first two films in the Die Hard Series. A lot of the movies we watched on team outings over the years.

Pete Carroll invited us all over for a barbecue during the summer. I think I was a freshman. It was a scheduled easy day, but as many crazy workout days as there were, there were rest days to goof off, too. Pete's father, Ed, was active with the group and a runner himself. I remember running 10k races along side of him as I was growing up through the junior ranks. He and Pete's mom, Iris, had a farm along Jockey Hollow Road and to this day, I still remember that as one of the most enjoyable summer afternoons I ever had as a kid.

All of us runners, boys team, girls team, more than a few parents and adults, turned up and we played what must have been two hours of ultimate frisbee in their front field. Back and forth. Throwing and catching. Running everywhere and it was as good a workout as any ten or twelve miler.

We ended up adopting that as an alternate workout from time to time through the summers to keep things interesting. On the high school football field, we'd play barefoot which we decided was a great way to build strength in our feet.

This past spring here in Colorado, at a community event, we met a young man named Duncan Atherton who was excited to learn Aiden was coming out for the Niwot High School team. He described it as serious, but really, really fun. And how when you're on the team, you never have to worry about having someone to eat lunch with in the cafeteria. Or a ride. Or someone just to hang out with. They really are a family that way, Duncan said. And it threw me back to this specific party at the Carroll's farm. We were all hanging out together. Freshman like me and Jeff on up to college guys like Pete and Buck. And Mrs. Carroll put out a spread of food for us all to enjoy.

That was team life in a nutshell. We'd do movie nights in the fall on the nights before big races. Usually a Rocky or a Lethal Weapon. Something action-oriented. We'd have team outings. They didn't have to be mandatory, we just loved doing things together.

I sometimes wonder what my life would have been like if I didn't have a team and people like this around me growing up. I was a shy, sort of geeky kid. I could talk with anyone, but starting a conversation, that was something else entirely. I preferred talking to the adults more than kids my own age. To think about starting a conversation with one of the girls—that was completely intimidating.

These people, all of them, became another family to me. And whether they know it or not, I learned so, so much from them every day.

From the older guys who I often wanted to be.

The way Rory Farrell raced across the Polo Grounds.

The way John Carlotti committed to training.

The way Chris Blanchet talked to people. Anybody.

The inexhaustible cool of Paul Stogryn.

The confidence of Hallinan.

The generosity of Pete Carroll (and kindness of his dad, Ed. And sweetness of his mom, Iris.)

And just being around the girls. Getting to know them like regular human beings and teammates, too. Even now, I'm almost always up for a game of Ultimate. Any time.

# Legacy Lost

## 12

> "My name is Ozymandias, King of Kings.
> Look on my Works, ye Mighty, and despair."
> - P.B. Shelly, 1817

They say records are made to be broken. It's certainly true in sport, but in so many other things in life as well. We time our races so we can see who wins—and who compares to other people running the same distance and who ran it best on certain courses 100 years ago. We time our runs and workouts so we can compare our efforts to ourselves. How fast we did it last time. How we did compared to when we were young. A losing proposition by any measure. Time always wins out.

But we time things for other reasons, too. We do it to honor the sport and the time we spent doing the sport and when. And so we—the people watching the sport can remember. World records. National records. Meet records. Age group records. And they're all kept by the most passionate among us. Tucked away in hand-written notebooks enshrined on a shelf in a home library somewhere. In places like Eugene and Boulder and San Jose and New York and Clinton and Bernardsville. And we remember the records both formal and informal, and the days we saw them set. The temperatures and the wind. Or was it still? The rain or snow or rawness of it all. Was it a calm spring day or mud up to the ankles? A close match with three or five other runners or she ran away from everyone from the gun and left them all struggling far behind?

The records were made to be broken, but the stories were told to be passed on. Onto the next. To remember, sure, but also to inspire. To get more of us to share the passion. To honor the sport and the practitioners of the sport. The best whoever ran, jumped, and threw. But also to install those moments into human history. To share the smaller, just as important bits to other human beings so they are honored as well and don't disappear from the world. These moments in time that would otherwise be left forgotten in an old log book filled with slippery handwriting and eventually tossed in a bin as unimportant paper when the parents' house gets packed up and sold.

I used to be able to recite the world record for the mile run from Said Aouita's 3:46.7 in Helsinki in 1987 back to Paavo Nurmi's 4:10.4 in 1923. I was there for Eamonn Coughlin's first sub-3:50 indoors. And all of those digits are engraved in the record books as they should be.

But I also remember the summer day Thomas Praisner ran 1:57 for our 20 Course. The fastest any of us could remember. Faster than John Carlotti. Faster than Brad Hudson. Waaay faster than me. I remember the cool, breezy day I ran 4:08 for 20 x 100m. Under 12.5 for each and faster than Carlotti or Nielsen ever ran that workout. I remember my teammates and I running 10:16 for the distance medley on a blustery day inside the West Point field house in 1985. The fastest time of the year by any high school team and second fastest indoors, only to Bernards '82 at the same venue where, according to the Star-Ledger, Paul Stogryn ran a "scintillating" 3:06 opening 1200m leg. They ran 10:12 that day. A national indoor record for school boys at the time.

It was cold, windy, and snowy. The same way it always was when we drove up to race indoors at the Military Academy field house overlooking that left turn in the Hudson River where George Washington strung anchor chains to blockade the British ships.

But it was a fast, firm, flat 200m track with big, wide turns and they ran a series of great meets through the winter. And we wanted, needed, to get a fast qualifying time for Penn a few months down the road. Mark took the 82/83 team there before that memorable drive down the last straightaway inside Franklin Field and we went there each of the next several. In 1985, the 10:16, I ran 4:12, my fastest indoor leg ever. But before we got there, we spent :45 minutes or more warming up only to find out two things:

1) there were four heats of the Distance Medley on the schedule; and

2) the fast heat, our heat, would go off last.

Four heats. 12-ish teams per heat. 40-50+ teams in this little meet up the river from the city. And with at least 20 minutes each and 10-ish minutes between, the race we were ready for NOW, would not step to the line for almost two more hours. 6:03 longer for me as the anchor. So we had the longest warm-up of all time. We just kept jogging around and back and forth inside the field house. We got to know every ripple and fold in the track surface better than anyone. But it must not have hurt in the end.

Legacy is a fancy, important-sounding word for "what people remember." But it fits. In music, they call it influence. As in, asking the latest chart-topper "who are your musical influences?" Like Clapton came from Muddy. And Chuck and Howlin' Wolf gave us Keef. Then Buddy Guy showed Stevie Ray how to get where he went. They not only inspired with their playing and recordings, because recordings were new-fangled at one time, they would take them under their wings or compete with them. Clapton and Keef and Stevie knew and played and performed with Muddy and Chuck and Howlin' Wolf and Buddy. And that's where the secret lies. The person-to-person. Where legacy diverges from lineage.

You don't inherit it. You learn it and earn it from those willing to teach you.

I wasn't there that day in Bernardsville, but I've heard the story so many times I need to wish I was. It was before my time. In the late-1970s—I don't know the year or even time of year exactly. I think it was the summertime. Arthur Lydiard came to Bernardsville. The great coach who changed everything. It was at the invitation of Larry Sullivan. Retired Air Force Colonel. Commercial pilot. Friend of all of us who ran in Bernardsville. Parent of several kids in the program including John Sullivan who ran 3:00 on the 1979 Penn team. Close friend of both Ed Mather and Mark Wetmore. Closer than anyone. When I think of what the word "friendship" means—for real—I think of the way Mark and Larry interacted with each other. To have one friend in your life like Larry Sullivan, you are very lucky, indeed.

"Larry's influence reverberated through my work for 45 years," Mark told me once.

According to the version of the story I know, these three met; Arthur, Larry, Mark, and talked. And Arthur listened, and taught. And they went out for a run that would become famous to us. Thirty miles through the Somerset Hills countryside. The great man of our sport from New Zealand who coached Snell to so much Olympic glory and so many others. Proud of his accomplishments, but always celebrating the athletes. Always more of an evangelist, or prophet, than ever any kind of glory hound. The man who believed there are champions all around us, they just need the proper training.

He thrived on sharing his passion for the sport and he understood how it should be done. There's a lot of time for questions and answers on a hilly, 30-mile run.

The three men hung together the entire way talking, Wetmore after a better understanding of how to apply Lydiard's concepts to young people, new runners, as they grow. Ten to 14-year-old Junior Olympic Club runners require different things than high school runners who require different things than college athletes and runners with some experience. And that day, over what would become the famed 20-Course plus 10 miles, was when it all truly began.

Teeny, tiny Bernards High School was an outsized influence on distance running before this time. Ed Mather came to Bernards in 1964 and started having an impact right away. Rich Axtell finished 9th in the first-ever New Jersey cross-country All-Groups meet. What would become the Meet of Champions. The earliest of 23 state group championships and the beginning of a reputation that would eventually be understood as odd, flamboyant, confrontational, straight-shooting, and most important, inspirational. To look for the magic of Wetmore in establishing a desire to show up for training, you need look no further.

That is how I understood the idea of legacy. So many lessons formal and mostly not. Intentional and sometimes accidental. Experiential learning from the people who inspire you most and teach you how to pay attention to what's important. How to experiment without fear. How to put it all into action. And how to do the same for others.

I don't think there's anyone who knows anything about our sport who would argue that Mark Wetmore is one of the most successful developmental coaches in history. Sure, he's been great for the runners who were champions before they met him. But he's taken so many high school and college runners of mid-level performance to massive success.

In the old days, even as recent as my college days, the standard M.O. at just about every college—frankly, in almost any sport—was...
A) get the most talented batch of athletes you can find signed up.
B) Run them to death 400m repeat after another til they drop.
C) On race day, run whoever is healthy enough to make it around the course.

It was an objectively ridiculous method.

So many coaches learned that way they seemed to want or need to take out that same kind of suffering on others. The attitude was "I did it this way, why should I change?" Even if all your best guys and girls are hurt and can't get to the start line, let alone the finish. It's the way it was always done, so the method hung on and on and on until somebody found something better.

That legacy isn't a direct straight line, though. Anyone looking for a simple answer or who suffers from overtly magical thinking will be disappointed.

It's sort of a family tree diagram but branch out where there are more than two parents.

Maybe it's an environment that creates a batch of believers. A group spawns another group? It's a puzzle with pieces that don't always seem to fit together. A journey. A trail. An ecosystem.

I ran with Mark Wetmore, well. Then I went to Charlie Jenkins at Villanova and never adjusted. Where there was no "system," or plan, or method at all. So I only understood one school of coaching. All directly evolved from the Lydiard approach. So maybe I'm less flexible than some.

On another hand. A more contemporary hand. I watch the work my son is doing this summer at Niwot High School with Coach Kelly Christensen and there is absolutely a system in place. A method to the training that the young athletes follow and understand and trust. One that has significant differences from the one I grew up with, but Christensen has them bought-in. The one thing that's exactly the same is that they all love to be there with him and with each other every day. They do some things I'm not used to like specificity work all year long and hill sprints in June before the heavy summer training gets going in earnest. But they do some things I do recognize like measuring in minutes instead of miles the way Lydiard preferred. Like Wetmore's, it is a system that gets undeniable results. And I trust that Aiden and his teammates are in very good hands.

There's no one way to do things. And different athletes respond to different stimuli. Which, by the way, is a cornerstone of everything I learned from Mark Wetmore. Training concepts in a steady state of adaptation. Legacy is about the environment.

It's not a biblical begat environment. One coach birthing the next. It's evolution. Influence. Adaptation. Necessity.

And there are unique approaches that shove it all forward.

Some things nudge gently. Other things are so radical, they kick 100-year-old doors down. There are many, many things I learned from Mark that I still think about every day. Truly. Every day.

# WORKOUT: Summer Ks

After putting in the miles for weeks on end, we start to transition to faster things. We always did slight downhill strides along the school parking lot after our runs. Even in the early summer. The slight downhill was to teach your legs to run faster than normal and facilitate that turnover that would come in handy not just at the end of races, but up hills as well. Then we would do the following two workouts on alternate weeks, usually a Tuesday or Wednesday. Once or twice a summer.

Always warm-up and warm-down, 2-3 miles on each end of the workout.

### THE WORKOUT: 6 X 1,000M

1 x 1,000m @ xc race pace.
800m interval at standard training pace.
Repeat six times to get 6,000m @ xc race pace.
Total: 10,000m

Time the duration of the workout AND each 1,000m repeat for pace, sweltering in the New Jersey summer sun.

## THE WORKOUT 8 X 600M

1 x 600m @ xc race pace.

400m interval at standard training pace.

Repeat eight times to get a total of 8,000m. 4,800m at race pace. About 5 miles.

Time the duration of the workout AND each 600m repeat for pace. Then hang at The Wall with the brother/sisterhood.

# Riding with the King

# 13

"See yourself - You are the steps you take
You and you, and that's the only way
Shake, shake yourself - You're every move you make
So the story goes."

- Yes.

**APRIL 3, 1986.**

"Yeah!" Mr. Mather said with a vague sense of recognition. "You look good. Good to see you. Lost some hair!"

He was chatting with a fellow driver in the rest area who recognized him from his high school days and all of the boys completely broke up into the kind of laughter you remember forever.

We'd just climbed back on the yellow minibus at a roadside rest stop on Route 95 somewhere in the Commonwealth of Virginia on our long journey from the Bernards High School parking lot to the Motel 6 on the Richmond Road in Williamsburg, Virginia.

Mr. Mather was our driver and regular entertainment. Seven hours south was a long time to spend aboard a rickety short bus filled to the brim with bags of gear, Walkmen, pillows, stadium blankets, a couple of boom boxes because—music—we never went anywhere without it. And a bunch of overly hormoned teenagers.

The Colonial Relays was one of the premier pre-Penn Relay meets in the country—certainly the Mid-Atlantic region in those days. We were tuning up for our run at a Penn watch and took a pair of boys distance medley crews down for a run-off.

Ten boys and six girls, runners and throwers riding together with Mr. Mather behind the wheel. We were never so frightened in our lives. He drove the way he spoke—with inspiration, aspiration, confidence, and excitement. And occasionally a little doziness. We took bets on which lane we were supposed to be in.

We ran into a young father driving with his family along the way who recognized him. Ran for him back in the 70s. That was the line about his hair. Mr. Mather remembered him with the long hair of his generation. Knowing him the way he obviously did, the guy smiled good naturally and went on his way, taking no offense from his old coach—traveling north with his wife and kids. We never caught his name.

Arrived in the dark on Thursday scheduled to run Friday afternoon.

I was lost in a mist of unrequited teen love that weekend. Broken up with—dumped by—unceremoniously by my first real girlfriend that winter. On the same teams and around each other all the time, so that was inconvenient. She was on the Virginia road trip, too. Also a less than optimal thing for my sense of well-being.

They write songs about all of these feelings. The Blues and Rock & Roll both built on break-up songs. Plays and books and poems, too. And notes to be passed between friends in school hallways and lunch rooms. It's such a natural part of growing up we all understand it.

"She likes you."

"LIKES me, likes me? Or just likes me."

"I think she Likes you."

Looking back from adulthood it's all so cute and funny and trite and nostalgic. But in the moment, it is everything. It changes gravity and reverses tides and helps you learn those obsessive compulsive things we all need to learn in our lives before we grow up into the bigger things. When puppy love dissolves and the real thing rears its head.

I remember as the little yellow bus pulled into Williamsburg past all the fast-food places Ranjan was obsessively excited to hit the Taco Bell a couple of doors down once the bus door opened and let us off. He felt the gravitational pull of Tex-Mex since he'd moved from Naperville and realized we didn't break for the border much in the Garden State. The idea was immediately vetoed by Mark who directed us to Morrison's Cafeteria. A totally forgettable meal with the notable exception of my first-ever hush puppies. Morrison's was probably a better choice for our digestion with a big race the next day.

**FRIDAY AFTERNOON. APRIL 4, 1986.**

**THREE WEEKS TO PENN.**

Still not sure who was going to run which leg three weeks from now, and committed to not making any of the same mistakes as last year, we split our team at Colonial.

**Red Team** - Jeff Simpson, Andy Burgess, Brad Bono, Ranjan Sinha

**White Team** - Thomas Praisner, Greg Mallek, Jeff Friedman, Lyle Smith

It was an A and a B team that day. Red team and white team, actually, and we all had different things to prove. Simpson, I think, was trying to get more comfortable in his role as leadoff man. With John

Sullivan's 3:00 in '79 and my 3:04 in '84, we had strong history at that oddball distance. Ranj was a complete fish out of water on the Red team anchor leg, but competitive fellow that he was, it wasn't in his nature to lose.

Andy Burgess was quarterback of the Mountie football team who ran the 400m leg on the snakebit '85 team and Greg Mallek was a national, if not, world-class musician. They were friends, but battling for the sprint spot on the team.

Then Thomas Praisner, Jeff Friedman and Brad Bono. Juniors staking out claims on the 4th slot of the 4 x 800m team. All three could go under 2:00 on any given day. But this was the day.

And me. I was tuning up for my job in Philly. I was ready, but really just trying to get and stay sharp and keep my head focused on my job and not my love life or lack thereof. And as competitive as Ranjan was, I had no intention of losing either.

Not to mention the other 10 or 12 teams from Virginia, Maryland, North Carolina, Pennsylvania, Delaware and New York eager to show off and eat up the track inside the red bricks of the William & Mary stadium.

After the gun, the team of Simpson, Burgess, Bono got the stick to Sinha 15 or 20m up on me and the others. We were just about exactly where Mark expected us to be when I jumped out ahead of Friedman too early. He reached out to pass me the stick just as I turned to bolt quicker than I should have. I felt him drop the red aluminum tube between my shoulder blades and it rolled down my back falling right into my fingers. I gripped the smooth, cool metal before it hit the ground and took off on my assignment. Step-by-step, I started to eat up the space between me and my friend, wondering if I had enough real estate to catch him. I did with about 300m to go and went by him behind the grandstand set up inside the far turn with less than 200m left. I broke the tape at 10:21 with our second foursome just a few steps behind in 10:23. Still two of the fastest times of the year to date and our lineup for Penn was set.

## SATURDAY AFTERNOON. APRIL 5, 1986.
## 4 X 800M. NEXT DAY.

The team: Simpson, Bono, Sinha, Smith

We always seemed to put so much focus on the Distance Medley, it was easy to forget we had a really competitive 4 x 800m team almost every time we took to the track. As you might expect, people noticed that we took first and second in the Distance Medley on Friday—reactions among the competition swung from impressed to intimidated to annoyed. Whether that means the other 4 x 8 teams were looking at Saturday as an opportunity or a threat was outside of my control, but I felt nothing but a sense of inevitability. We had an incident-free trip around the track with everybody doing their exact job and hit the tape first just under 7:50.

So two races. Two firsts and a second. The girls ran well. The throwers performed well. And we were walking around happy in our noticeable red sweats, talking to anyone who wanted to say hello or rehash the competition.

Thomas, Ranjan, and I were walking across the infield toward the concession stand when we were approached by what appeared to be an angry leprechaun. Short, agitated, and pissed, he addressed me directly.

"I haven't heard back from any of my letters I wrote to you," was the only thing I could make out of a string of fiery conviction.

The first weeks of spring are stressful for student athletes. At least that was the truth in 1986.

Acceptance letters and rejections and wait-list letters had mostly all arrived in the mail. We still used the mail back then. Those of us who'd already signed letters of intent were trying to finish the school year and spring season off strong. Others were waiting on offers of scholarships or just thick acceptance packets from the dream schools where they'd spend the next four years of their lives.

My friend Ranjan was stressed and depressed. His father was a world-class physicist. His brother a gifted lifelong academic. And Harvard said no. And that was his primary goal. His lifelong touchstone—Cambridge. He didn't really have any other school he wanted to go to and was wandering through springtime crestfallen and a little aimless.

"I'm sorry, I don't know who you are," I said to this strange-looking man in a kelly green windbreaker and baseball cap.

"I'm Roy Chernock. Head coach here. And I sent you all sorts of letters to talk to you about coming to school here and..."

"I'm sorry coach Chernock. I never received anything from you."

We talked over each other a bit, him trying to get his point across to me. Me trying to calm him down enough to explain that I'd never received any recruiting letters from him.

"Where did you send them?" I asked.

"I sent them to Bernards High School, care of..."

Both of us together, "Mr. Mather."

Immediately, we understood. He calmed down, disappointed. It is unknown the reason, but I figured Ol' Ed didn't think I was a fit for W&M. Either that or he just lost them. Even money on which. I wouldn't even hazard a guess how many of us never saw recruiting letters that could have changed everything for us because of Ed Mather.

A calmed-down Chernock turned back into his normal good nature and we chatted a little bit about the meet and the school when he turned to look at Ranjan.

"Hey, you ran pretty great out there yesterday and today," he said pulling him under his wing. "Where are you going to school?"

In a moment or two, Chernock called Hiram Cuevas over telling him to take Ranjan on a running tour of the campus whispering to be sure to end up at the admissions office. Less than an hour later, Ranjan had toured William & Mary, got the insider scoop from the team's top miler, signed his name to a blank application and been accepted to attend the oldest college in America. In a week, he had a partial track scholarship and a dorm assignment. In four years, he had a varsity letter and degrees in math and physics and a plan to head west to Stanford for aerospace engineering.

It's funny how things work out sometimes.

Years later, Heather and I were stuck in traffic on the New York State Throughway coming back from a Catskills weekend. My phone was blowing up with messages that I only half-understood. Ranjan was living in Thailand and engaged and happier, I thought, than I'd seen him in a long time. The time zones meant we hadn't been in touch often. But apparently, something violent happened to him. He was attacked, or broken-into, or injured to the point of bleeding out in his apartment in Bangkok. He was gone. I sat in stalled traffic on the highway trying to process the information. I never quite understood the details, but the fact remained. Ranjan was gone. His dad and his brother, Arjun, traveled to scatter his ashes over the Ganges and near their home in San Diego. And I still think of his parents, Sunny and Loni who were like second parents to us, and hope they somehow can find some peace.

Mark went out of his way to sit alone with me high up in the William & Mary stands late that Saturday afternoon. We talked in round terms about important things like we'd done since that day in his white van after I'd run away from my first cross-country race.

He told me he was proud of the way I'd been able to focus this week with so much going on in my life. He could tell I was distracted. He made me feel confident, proud of myself for things outside of my running. Like I could tackle anything the world threw at me. And it's a feeling I've tried to carry with me ever since.

# WORKOUT: The Golf Course

In the latest Golf Digest list of the top 100 golf courses in the United States, Somerset Hills Country Club was ranked #57. It's always been a spectacular course and was a great place to work as a caddie when I was young. I presume it still is.

Ultra-private, but an important part of the history of Gilded Age Bernardsville, the club membership is made up of community-oriented athletics fans that always allowed the cross-country team to train around the perimeter of the course on Mondays in the fall. The course was closed for Caddie Day on Mondays with virtually no member traffic, so we were able to run the 2.5-mile hilly perimeter in the rough without causing any issue to anyone.

There were a variety of workouts we did on Mondays the day after our long runs. Usually, it was designed to get used to running on the grass and uneven terrain required for our sport. And often designed to get us used to running up-tempo at race pace or a bit faster.

We'd do one or two or three loops as the season wore on at 2-3 fartlek. That's two minutes on, three minutes off. Over and over again. Or 3-2 fartlek. Or as we neared racing season, we'd be up to three loops at 4-1 fartlek. Four minutes on. One minute off. Sometimes restarting mid-hill before looping around behind the clubhouse.

You couldn't do these workouts almost every week without adopting a fearlessness about cross-country running.

One-mile-ish warmup to the Golf Course.

3 Loops of 4-1 fartlek. 9-10 fast sections.

One-mile-ish warm-down back to school

Call it 10 miles.

# Things Change

## 14

"A big man knows the value of a small coin."
- From Things Change
by David Mamet & Shel Silverstein

I sometimes think I've been depressed since I was 19 years old. I was 100 percent sure I'd be an Olympian. 100 percent sure. In a world, I'd learn later, where nothing is 100 percent. Pretty sure I'd be a gold medalist. Nearly positive I'd be the next, fourth, high-schooler to break four minutes for one mile even though we didn't run that distance much anymore. I knew all the names and all the times. Ryun. Danielson. Liquori. It never occurred to me there may be some other under-18-year-olds in other parts of the world who'd done that, too. I was from the US My bedroom was papered in red, white, and blue wallpaper (mom's choice). And Liquori was the one. He was from Jersey. Not far from me. Essex Catholic. I was Catholic. He ran for Jumbo at Villanova. So that's where I wanted to go. Fred Dwyer was his coach in high school. Dwyer ran at Villanova—went on to coach at Manhattan College. Later, he sat in my parents' living room trying to cajole me into running for him. I couldn't be swayed. The romance of the white singlet with the navy lettering was too strong. Freddy didn't like it, but he understood.

Looking back, I probably should have listened. I should have listened to Wetmore, too. What he wasn't telling me. He never would have told me where to go to school. Probably even if I asked him directly. He knew how much I wanted Villanova. How hard I dreamed about it. I talked to Pete Carroll about it. He walked-on for Jumbo. Ran with Marcus. But dreams are only a part of it all. I dreamed of running for Jumbo. But Jumbo died in 1981. It would never be the same after that. It might have never been what I imagined it to be in the first place.

I think Mark would have preferred me to go out to run for Martin Smith at Wisconsin, something I'd never even considered. I had an Easterner's arrogance about midwestern places like Wisconsin. I sometimes wonder what would have happened if I'd gone West. Or if I'd asked if Villanova had a place for Mark. But that would have been an entirely different story. And maybe not a good fit.

I remember having a goal when I was a seventh-grader. Cross-country season went well. I won the Bernards Invitational and got 3rd in the TAC Supernationals in North Carolina in my age group. We finished at nationals in St. Louis. Three girls and me and a handful of parents. Mark and my dad and I went to watch the St. Louis Steamers indoor soccer team the night before the race. I ran competitively, but not spectacularly.

Spring came and my goal was sub 5:00 at the Bernards Track Invitational. It was our biggest meet of the season. Breaking 5:00 as a seventh grader was a big deal to me. There are faster now, but that was pretty quick in those days.

There's a picture of me leading the race on the back stretch. Black and white blown up in my dad's basement darkroom like so many of my favorite photos. I'm in front with JP just behind. Both of us in our Mine

Mountain Road Department singlets. And there's Jim Hopta from Ridge just behind us. We would become good friends over the years. He went to St. Joe's in Philly so we covered much of the same Main Line ground.

Mather Graduated from St. Joe's, too. But I don't remember him saying much about his time there.

Great memories. Great photo. Fell short on time and then the junior track season was over. We didn't have too many chances on the track in those days.

School ended and I wanted one more shot before I became an 8th grader.

That Saturday morning dawned cool and damp and misty in Bernardsville. I jogged down to the high school track alone to warm up. Just me in my "agony of da feet" 3/4 sleeve baseball shirt and blue striped sweat pants carrying my old Adidas spikes in my hands. I jogged around the track a few times running a few quick strides the way I'd been taught. I was stretching on the ground when I saw my dad walking down the parking lot to see me, his stop watch around his neck.

I didn't tell him my plan but he had a knack of knowing things. So not too surprised. He timed me with the watch from the real one-mile starting line. The one 9.3m behind the start/finish on the 400m oval. I asked him to call out splits each lap. I started my Casio wrist watch, too, just to be sure. I wouldn't want to have to try again.

Stripped down, spiked up, and sweating on the line the way Mark taught us, I was ready for my solo time trial. Three 75-second laps and a kick would do the trick. Runner set, go, and I was off around the first turn, the back stretch and the far turn back to where I'd started. It was weird running all alone. "74 - 75 - 76..." I heard going through the first lap. "2:28 - 2:29 - 2:30..." on the second. "3:42 - 3:43 - 3:44..." on number three and one hard lap to go. It was misty and I felt the sweat and water in my eyes on the back stretch. The 200m mark was the quietest, loneliest part of the Bernards track. Even on big meet days it seemed a million miles from everything. I hung on with everything I had trying to accelerate with every step. Kicking up and ducking my head to try and find another gear. Long view down the home stretch. 50m line under me. Just a few more steps.

I remember my dad showing me the face of the stopwatch after I finished. 4:57. Same as my Casio. Back to training tomorrow.

I was in the eighth grade a year later when I received my first college recruiting letter. Typed on a typewriter on athletic department stationery. Expressing interest in me. A young, junior high school student who finished top five in the Junior Olympic cross-country nationals. Ran about 4:40 for a mile. It was exciting, and surprising, and undoubtedly a violation of NCAA rules. It felt like a winning lottery ticket. or getting asked to the party by the girl you thought didn't know you existed. Or in Jersey terms, picking up a beautiful new watch that just fell off a truck. I had to wonder if they knew they were recruiting a class of eighth-graders.

I wasn't the only one getting recruiting letters. Tracey Hinman got her first a year before me. And she was a year younger. Over time, I heard from all sorts of schools and coaches. Big packet from LSU and Ole Miss. Rice University and Georgia Tech. The Naval Academy coach typed times and meets on the outside of the envelope. "9:38.9 3000m steeplechase," it said. "Frosh nat'l record." That's how I found out. Manhattan and Cornell and Ithaca. Princeton seemed interested which I should have paid more attention to, but I was arrogant and it was in New Jersey, like Rutgers and Rider and Rowan and… UVa caught my interest and I took a visit there. The only place I seriously considered other than where I ended up. I spent a lot of time on the phone—land lines, long distance calls—with Norm Levine at Brandeis. Small. Predominantly Jewish. Division 3. Brandeis named after a Supreme Court Justice. Great school. Wonderful man at the helm. I spent hours of time talking to him at Boston indoor meets, leaning on the high bank of the track at BU. He gave me so much good advice. Like another dad in a lot of ways. It hurt to disappoint him so. I probably would have done well there. But I had bigger ideas in my noggin.

If I had just a little more understanding of myself at the time—I should have looked further west. California would have been good for me. But I was afraid of going too far from home. I was a Jersey boy. I'm still a Jersey boy and will forever be.

My grandfather always wanted to send me to golf school in Florida when I was young. I thought maybe it was a joke at the time, but if you asked him—no! It absolutely was not. My parents—my mom didn't want any part of it. So I didn't go. Another lost opportunity that could have changed my life?

I loved my dad and my grandfather and never wanted to be away from them for too long. And my mom taught me nostalgia, which kept me near the things and places and people I knew.

And none of that—relying on that—crutching along with that—it didn't do anything to help me as an adult. It didn't make me a better person. Or a smarter person. It taught me to throw away that sense of adventure that could have made me more than I am.

Advice to you young runners out there—don't be afraid to break away. It could save your life. Or at least your long term sanity.

VanCortlandt Park 1979.

Colonial Relays 1986.

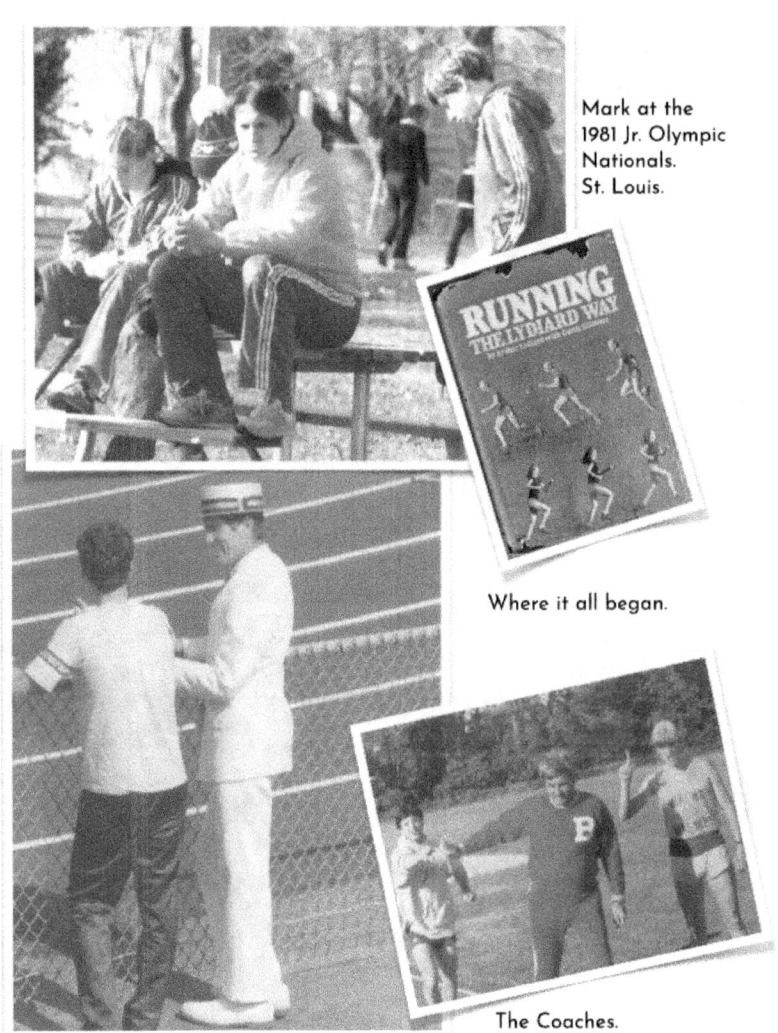

Mark at the 1981 Jr. Olympic Nationals. St. Louis.

Where it all began.

The Coaches.

Larry Sullivan in his Bernards Invitational-best.

Buck Logan running out Hardscrabble Rd. in the Waldron Memorial. Pete and Ed Carroll at right.

Buck Logan, Pete Carroll, Jim Nielsen, Jim Smith of Haddonfield in Asbury Park.

Fans & friends at the Bernards Invitational 1984.

John Carlotti outstepped in the Bernards Invitational 800m, 1982.

Chris Blanchet (above left) and Paul Stogryn (above right) in the 1983 Group I 3200m.

John Carlotti and Chris Blanchet at the Rutgers Relays 1983 in their new Zooms.

Larry Sullivan & Peter Carroll.

Mark at the gateway to the west, 1981.

Mark organizes the group onto the Kent Bus to the Utica Boilermaker.

In the papers. Making the New York Times in 1980 after capturing 100 consecutive dual meets.

The 1980 MMRD Jr. Olympic Team

The 1984 Bernards Mountaineers. (Front row) Peter Beckwith, Jim Nielsen, me. (Standing) Thomas Praisner, Mr. Mather, Jeff Simpson, Ranjan Sinha, Stephen Praisner.

The changing team. The 1980 Mine Mt. Road Dept. Junior Olympic Team (top) and the 1982 NJSIAA All-Groups Champions under our home base tree (center & bottom).

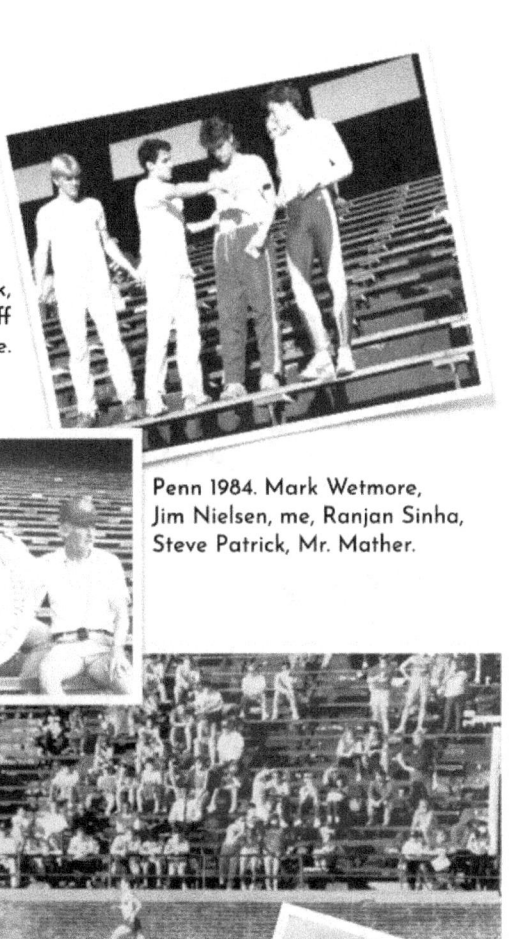

Penn 1986. Greg Mallek, Ranjan Sinha, Jeff Simpson, me.

Penn 1984. Mark Wetmore, Jim Nielsen, me, Ranjan Sinha, Steve Patrick, Mr. Mather.

Penn 1986.

Mark and me. 1980 TAC Supernationals, Raleigh, NC.

## CU

# 15

*"There are no beaten paths
to the heights of Mount Olympus."*

- Charles Mark Wetmore

**JUNE, 2024**

Gene Bartow replaced John Wooden at UCLA. How many people do you know who remember Gene Bartow, all due respect?

Letting Wetmore go was like letting John Wooden's contract expire.

There are coaches in NCAA history with longer records. More winning records. More national championships. Maybe even more Olympic and World Championship success. But what Mark Wetmore's teams accomplished in his 29-years as the head coach at the University of Colorado is an important chapter in American running history.

And what comes next may not be predictable, exactly, but without a reliable crystal ball, Wetmore's successor, Sean Carlson, is statistically more likely to be remembered on the list with Gene Bartow than the list with John Wooden.

Football... it's always about football. Or basketball. Or ticket sales. Or TV deals. Or now, NIL deals. There are a wide variety of details that could be to blame for the head track and cross-country coaching change at

CU in 2024. Things that I'll never know. I wasn't in those rooms. Very few people were. What I do know is there was a controversy about body composition testing that boiled down as far as I could see, to one young woman who didn't make the varsity, transferring, then years later complaining about how she was spoken to at CU. Curious to many of us that even though she made the team at her new school, all of her personal best times came at CU. Then there's the Coach Prime situation. Deion Sanders came to Boulder. And changed everything. I don't think there was any real, direct conflict with the track and cross-country teams, but Athletic Directors being bean counters. And beans being beans. And football being football. My guess is Rick George, the AD, made a call. There's a reason we remember and love the great athletes and the legendary coaches and not the great Athletic Directors.

Athletic Directors are not leaders. They are more… clerks. Some handle transitions well. Some do not.

## VILLANOVA UNIVERSITY - 1949-1981

James "Jumbo" Elliott, or Mr. Elliott as most people called him, stood in the south stands of Franklin Field dressed in his uniform—a tailored suit and tie—watching his runners compete and collect a ridiculous number of Championship of America watches from the University of Pennsylvania Relay Carnival during his career. He is universally considered a legend. His record includes:

- 8 NCAA Team titles in track and cross-country
- 82 individual NCAA crowns
- 66 world records
- 28 Olympians
- 5 Gold medalists

- 75 Penn Relays titles and 25% of the Distance Medley Championships of America in the 20th Century.

That's Yankees-level success.

Mr. Elliott was such a beloved figure. They put a statue of him on the new track standing with a stopwatch where he stood so many days of his life. Died in 1981. Legacy unexpectedly handed off to the next coach. Jack Pyrah stepped in to fill the gap. Charles Jenkins after that. There were some successes, but nothing like before. The women thrived under Marty Stern, but it would be some time before the mens' team found its balance again. Not until Marcus O'Sullivan returned to the Main Line as a coach.

## UNIVERSITY OF COLORADO - 1995-2024

Mark Wetmore stood on a hill away from all the hubbub as his men's and women's teams accepted the trophies and had their photographs captured in 2004 as NCAA National Cross-Country Champions. He had no interest in accolades. He let the young men and women of Colorado accept that for themselves and their school. He'd done the same with our high school teams. At CU, he coached to:
- 8 NCAA National Cross-Country Team Titles
- 26 Individual NCAA crowns
- 36 Conference team titles in cross-country
- 2 Conference team titles in track
- 110 Individual conference titles
- 10 Olympians (19 berths)
- 33 World Championship Team members
- 25 US World Cross-Country Team members (61 berths)
- 7 World Championship medals (2 Gold)

Rick George named Sean Carlson—Notre Dame, Tennessee—as Wetmore's successor in 2024 and it remains to be seen how the transition will go. To date, the mens' cross-country team made up of largely Carlson-recruited athletes and athletes who followed him from the University of Tennessee are ranked 17th in the nation in an underwhelming start. I've never met Carlson. I have no personal criticism. I hope he does well. The athletes, especially those who came to Boulder for Mark deserve it. The program's reputation deserves it. But history tells us transitions like this are very, very challenging. Gene Bartow had what would otherwise be judged tremendous success at UCLA if it wasn't just after John Wooden's time there. Only time, and the sportswriters, will tell.

Decisions made by clerks couldn't be designed better for failure and tossing legacy into the bin. The same kind of thing happened at Bernards High School. It took time and a little luck in getting a new coach with some vision to guide that program back to relevance. But high school is different. Isn't it? On another hand, Christian Brothers Academy of Lincroft just won it's 400th straight cross-country dual meet.

# Midnight

# 16

"Once I ran to you (I ran)
Now, I'll run from you
This tainted love you've given
I give you all a boy could give you
Take my tears and that's not nearly all
Oh, tainted love."

- Soft Cell,
Billboard Hot 100
NYE 1982

**M**y mom hosted a fancy New Year's Eve Party every year at #20 Stevens Street for years. Not quite black tie, but almost, the party welcomed guests from about 9 p.m. to well after midnight and served a menu of hot hors d'oeuvres and drinks. She was proud of her parties and excited when she was surprised by her guests' plus ones. Being Bernardsville, she had numerous people of influence and power unexpectedly come through the 40-50-guest shin digs from time to time. Bill Moyers. Malcolm Forbes. When Emily and I were little, we'd hide at the top of the stairs to watch all the adults drinking champagne and eating little, fancy food listening in on their adult conversations.

Later, I loved having an excuse to get out with the guys, instead.

The bus left the high school parking lot promptly at 8:30 p.m. We were all dressed for the weather. Layers and sweats and hats and painters gloves. And bags with our racing shoes. It was December 31st and just a few, short hours from the new year.

New Years Eve 1982 turning to 1983, the Mine Mountain Road Department took a bus of 30 or more runners into Manhattan for the New York Road Runners Club annual Midnight Run through Central Park.

The five-mile race through mainly the dark of night was a celebration. "Midnight" started at 11:59:59 so you can run into the new year. Instead of a starting gun, you get a volley of fireworks and you can hear the shouting and cheering from downtown in Times Square all the way up at Tavern on the Green.

There were people running in costumes and serious runners alike. They had "champagne stops" for the adults instead of water stops to ring in the new year. I remember running through nearly pitch black sections of the park with other runners and then seeing the leaders coming back toward me after the turnaround. It was cold. There were hats and gloves. We ran hard, and we had an absolute blast every time. Another invention of Mark's, there was always some new way to fold out running into our regular lives.

Pete Carroll invited a friend and teammate John Keyworth from Villanova home for the holiday and he joined us at Midnight running with us and riding the bus in and out of the city. My mom made sure for me to pass along her invitation to the team to come to the house for some food after we got back from the city.

The race was over for most of us by 12:45 a.m. We piled back on the bus and navigated the traffic downtown and out the Lincoln Tunnel back to Bernardsville. Not the whole group, but a pack of 15 or 20 of us wandered into my house after 2:00 a.m. and starving. With his English accent, my mom practically adopted Keyworth as she made sure we all had enough bite sized foods to satisfy our post-race appetites. All family. All welcome. All the time.

# WORKOUT: 300m Chasers

I haven't spoken in person to Jim Nielsen probably since he graduated in 1984. But I still consider him a great and true friend. He moved out to Illinois for his college at Northwestern. He now lives somewhere in Texas. We chat on email, more often recently, and I know a bit about his family, his wife, his kids, his career. He's still the kind of guy I'd love to have nearby to see at least at meets or races or community events from time to time.

When we were in high school together, we were great teammates and I felt a lot of love among us. But I was also two full years younger than he was. To be honest, he was probably more closely connected to the Blanchet's and the Stogryn's than he was to Ranjan and me even though we shared a Penn Relays experience so few have.

Summer training leading into the 1983 cross-country season was tough for me. I was caddying and tired of the 20-miler. Jim was our captain and pushed me to be a part of everything. My sophomore year was maybe my best running year ever, but I pushed back on Jim early and often. He was feeling a ton of pressure as far as I could tell. I presume it was to follow up on Carlotti's success the previous year. It was all self-focused and it came out against us running around him. There was conflict at practice. There was conflict on the bus. And nobody wanted to be off the bus.* He struggled with the pressure all cross-country season and while he ran very fast, indeed, I don't think he managed to hit all the goals he set for himself that season. I wish I could have understood it all better at the time. Maybe I could have been helpful, instead of the needling, little pain in the ass I remember myself being. I wasn't outwardly confrontational. Never was. Which was probably worse to a guy like Jim Nielsen.

Success isn't only about finishing first. The last Bernards invitational was in October 1983. It was the biggest invitational cross-country meet in the state with dozens of buses filling the parking lot at the municipal pool and hundreds of runners freshman to JV to Varsity spilling out all over the fields and trails every year to show their fitness at the beginning of the season.

Mark always said our home course was exactly one minute faster than Holmdel. Jim had put away a tremendous summer training season and was ready to lace up his flats to show what he had around the multiple loops of grass and Macadam up on Seney Drive. In the end, he crossed the line in 14:59, one of the fastest ever to circumnavigate the course and gathered confidence heading into The Easterns and The Manhattan College Invitational, and the state meet series.

I remember coming off the fields and down the pool road for the second time and Mark standing there at the phone pole that marked two miles shouting to me "you got a good one going today! Tough as nails! Tough as nails!" and taking that all the way up Seney Drive, dropping Andy Ball from Pequonnock, making the turn back toward the trail and hammering my way home to a third place finish. One of my most memorable races ever that I'm still proud of today. 15:23 on the home course, just third place, but feeling like a real cross-country runner.

In the end, the fall didn't work out the way Jim expected. But we all turned our attention to the indoor season and preparing for the Penn

Relays. Our friend and 400m man Steve Patrick wrote a great memoir of his experience on that team. I hope I can convince him to share it publicly some time.

But most of that indoor season, it was Jim and me and Ranjan and Steve hanging out after practices and on the bus and passing batons back and forth wherever we ran. I don't think the rest of the state or region really thought of us as a threat for Penn. But they weren't hanging with us all winter.

I spent most of my time chasing after Jim Nielsen in our workouts. It was rare that we ran together as a twosome and even rarer that I ran ahead of him on anything. Jim was one of the toughest work-horses I ever saw. Even the commitment John Carlotti showed leading up to the 1982 cross-country season—the training he did that knocked almost a minute off his time at Holmdel—was not equal to what Jim did every day.

One day, Mark gave us a workout for just the two of us. We were leading into the Group I championship and were tuning up the speed for a fast finish by any unknown challengers.

We did a series of 300m repeats. Eight of them.

We were to imagine about :47 second per 300m pace.

We would each lead alternate repeat; and

We each had 15 steps to pass the other guy once in every 300m.

No more. No less. One chance every time. Just get the jump on the other guy before he could react. The same way you'd move in a race. I got him once. He didn't get me at all.

I ended up getting the jump on him once more inside Rutgers Stadium for the 1,600m title in the Group I meet which surprised even me. My first state title.

Less than a week later in the Meet of Champions at South Plainfield, Jim won the 3,200m going away, then came back for a double attempt in the 1,600m. I was leading with about 300m to go, then Jim and what seemed like the entire world went by me storming for the finish. He won both races, then went on to run 4:07 at IPI in Chicago. Fastest mile of any Bernards runner ever.

* *The Electric Cool-Aid Acid Test,* by Tom Wolfe.

# Traut

# 17

*"The friend is the man who knows all about you, and still likes you."*

- Elbert Hubbard

I was still wearing my red Bernards Recreation t-shirt the first time I raced at Van Cortlandt Park.

It was 1691, 288 years earlier, when a Dutch merchant called Jacobus Van Cortlandt purchased the more than 1,100 acres of Bronx property that would become inextricably tied to his name.

Born at the southern tip of Manhattan Island in 1658, Jacobus was spared the title of immigrant by being born in a small Dutch settlement called New Amsterdam. The boy grew into a man of his time and made his way to wealth as a merchant, slave owner, and politico serving two terms as Mayor after new Amsterdam transformed into New York City. Grandfather of founding father John Jay, Jacobus' impact on American Distance Running and public golf is direct and fundamental even if he never envisioned such things in his lifetime.

Jacobus' family sold the property to to the city in 1888 as a growing part of New York's public park system project. The Van Cortlandt Park Golf Course opened as a 9-holer in 1895—it remains the oldest public golf facility in the country. It wasn't long before the golf course was used for cross-country races. The courses we still use today were laid out in 1915 and almost since, the park has played weekend host to teams of collegiate and high school runners pitting their best efforts against each other. Not to mention clubs of cricketers, ruggers (rugby players), baseball players, football players (both American and soccer), Gaelic footballers, Irish hurlers and dog walkers.

The massive flat field that makes up the main part of the park you can see is called The Parade Ground. It is 66 acres of sporting fields and running trails—6 baseball diamonds, five soccer pitches, a dozen cricket pitches, space for Gaelic football, grounds for a dozen cricket games at once, all laid out on the flat space between Broadway and the tall, stoney Vault Hill named for the cemetery there. At 1,146.43 acres, Vanny is New York City's third-largest park and an absolute Mecca of cross-country running.

It has survived threats over the years from gun play on the links at the south end to Robert Moses' transportational/environmental abuse of the property in the 30's at the north end. (See Robert Caro's extraordinary and sprawling book *The Power Broker* for a deeper understanding of the good, the bad, and the ugly of that effing guy.) From the near bankruptcies of all major American cities in the mid-1970s to the "improvements" made from the 80s to now. Some good. Some less-so.

But the endurance of Vanny as a running venue is undeniable. The love we all feel for the place runs deep. It is the first time I ever saw rugby, cricket, and Gaelic football played. On the same day. In the same view.

I have no evidence that old Jacobus intended all of this athletic joy as the legacy for his "Yonkers Plantation," but I believe it to be true that this flawed man of his time designed it to be so. Maybe to make up for his and his family's sins of the merchant class.

⇐ ⇒

My first visit to Vanny was 1979. for the New York Road Runner's Club National Youth Meet. Mark told us stories that brought the place to life even before we got there—the way he always did. The place was overwhelming and scary to an 11-year-old in that uniquely Bronx way. My sister, Emily, was dancing with with American Ballet Theater so I'd been into the city often by then, but that was midtown Manhattan driving with my mom through the Lincoln Tunnel. The George Washington Bridge across the Henry Hudson Parkway to park parallel on Broadway alongside Van Cortlandt in the Bronx was something different altogether.

The midget course was only a mile and a half. Same distance we ran on The Polo Grounds. It started at the high school starting line near the golf course side. It ran straight across the massively wide field to the cow path and shrunk from infinite to two across. Straight out and up and around to the bridge the long courses crossed onto the back loop. This course swept right back down the hill onto the cinder path to the finish line. A long, long, straightaway on the cinders. It was totally new to me, but felt so, comfortable. So familiar. The black and white picture my dad took of me in all red and bright white Adidas flats is one of my favorites of me. Everything is so fresh and new with only joy, no expectation. No memory of where I finished, but I remember Mark being satisfied.

Same course the next year. The longer, 3,000m course the third year was a new experience. Our first time roaring up the infamous Cemetery Hill past ol' Jacobus' final resting place. Always felt a bit Legend-of-Sleepy-Hollow to me. And it was the first time I met John Trautmann. What were we, 13?

I went into that race with a certain, I thought, earned confidence. All the miles and hills and speedy stuff. The fartlek and springing and bounding. I was ready and couldn't wait to get back to Vanny. After the gun, I found myself pawing my feet through the loose sand of the cow path beside this other kid. Shorter than me, but running well. We turned left toward the cemetery and I knew the Bernardsville Mountain had me set to take over. We started climbing and dropped the rest of the field, but this guy wouldn't go. Wouldn't drop. In fact, maybe halfway up, he attacked the hill passing me easily.

This is how I met John Trautmann who would go on to set the national high school 3000m record, make the 1992 Olympic team, set a world record with the Georgetown Distance Medley Relay team at Penn and become the head coach of the Empire Elite Track Club and NYU.

I remember saying out loud "you're gonna die." Of course, I'd done the work. There wasn't anyone else who could hammer up this short-ish, steep-ish hill with me. Nobody. He ran up and over, swung left at the bridge toward home. Away from me. I was flummoxed and going into oxygen debt. "What happened?" The whole thing I was so certain of was slipping away on the back of this kid I didn't know. I let my body fall forward encouraging gravity to carry me down onto the field below. Then I started lifting my knees—thinking like a track man. I spotted the back of the neck of that guy. I had to go get him. I felt my strides reach out long. I started to see him get closer—gobbling up the lead with every step. There, ahead was the banner over the finish with Kurt Steiner of the NYRR Club announcing the events of the day. I recognized the diminutive, round man running around the official space as the same man, minus his tuxedo, from the infield of the Millrose Games at Madison Square Garden. His thick, German accent calling me toward that finish line.

He was coming back to me, the little guy who wouldn't take die to heart by the old cemetery. I was sure he was coming back to me. I raced down the smooth, flat, cinder path with everything I had, sure I was going to catch him. And then, and then, and then, it was over. We'd crossed the line with me in a position I'd feel again on Fifth Avenue a few years later, like I could reach out and touch him on the shoulder. Damning the metric system, sure that if it was two miles instead of 3,000m, I would have been able to race my way ahead of him.

Second place is a big deal in a race like that—when you're young—it's a good thing. Second place at Van Cortlandt is success. When you're that young, second place is a stepping stone to what's next. But when you're sure of who you are and what you can do, second place stinks.

I congratulated him. Shook hands and high-fived some of the other kids. Then I found my dad chit-chatting with John's dad out past the finish line near the rugby pitch. They were kibitzing like old friends. I liked John's dad. He was always friendly to me. I liked John for the same reason. Even as the disappointment made part of me want to be dark and vindictive, I found it was not in my nature to be that. I guess I was raised well. I was more embarrassed by what I'd said struggling up the hill a few minutes before. "You're gonna die." Shouted with such assurance. As if it was just a natural inevitability. I wonder even now if Traut remembers that. He seemed to take energy from it at the time. It felt like I'd shouted. It might have been a whisper. It was, and remains, something I'm not proud of and maybe that's silly from so long ago. Something I never did before or since. And if he remembers it, even if he doesn't. If he ever reads this, there's a memory of a 13-year-old boy who'd like a chance to say he's sorry for acting the jerk on Cemetery Hill.

The lesson: never presume you're better than anyone until you drop them for good. And keep your opinions to yourself.

The next year, I was fortunate enough to win the same meet as a 14-year-old. I was a freshman who may or may not make the Bernards Varsity. It was my first win at Vanny. And my best run there.

## SEPTEMBER 1985

## THE DAY OF THE FIFTH AVENUE MILE

Drive into the city. Park somewhere on the street. You could do that in those days in the a.m. before people started turning up from the outskirts. When the native Manhattanites were coming from church and heading to brunch.

Wait for the high school race feeling very important and nervous.

Warm up.

Dad stood next to two secret service guys on the park side of the street maybe 250m from the finish at 60th St. not far from the bottom of the park. They were keeping an eye on one of the consulates. I don't know which one, nor would they have told me if I asked. But my dad spotted the lapel pins and the ear pieces and recognized them for who they were.

The start was near The Met. There were mounted police there and I liked looking at the horses. They calmed me, somehow. The start was downhill slightly for the first quarter mile. Then a slight rise to a view all the way to the finish line under the tree-lined sidewalk on the park side. Trautmann got a two or three meter lead on me as we crested the little rise and a breeze caught me in the chest. I was a six foot one inch tall spinnaker of a runner, taller than most of the others in most of my races, and lost another step or two on him. I remember he was on the left side of the double yellow and I was under the trees on the right. Maybe he knew something I didn't having won this a year before. I tried desperately with every remaining step to catch up. My yellow Adidas racers streaking along the city street—or so I imagined. It felt like that day digging my spikes into the ancient cinders of Van Cortlandt. Catching him until I wasn't anymore. Ten meters at that speed is about a second and a half. John raced through in about 4:06. Somehow, my hand-timed result got jotted down as 4:10.5. I watched the NYRR official gawping at the winner, then turning to me after I'd crossed. I was standing still in front of this fat man and watched him stop his watch at least a couple of seconds late, then read 4:10.5 to his cohort with the clip board. It was wrong. But official, so I'm officially a 4:10 guy. Unofficially is in my head...

My teammate on the girls side, Karen Ahearn finished second that day, too. My friends were there cheering us on and watching the elite results as they raced down the city street. Frank O'Mara from Ireland and a former Arkansas Razorback won the men's race.

We had a small bite, then piled into the cars to drive up to Vanny for a workout.

Simulation fartlek twice around the 2.5-mile high school course.

## SIMULATION FARTLEK

"Fartlek" is Swedish for "speed play" and it's an old, trusted method of training. It's also a very funny word, so fill in your own personal flatulence joke here. Mark invented something he called "simulation fartlek" where you would run race pace (or faster) for a specific distance of a course, then stop the watch at that point. Jog around a bit, then start the watch where you left off. Over and over again, collecting the fast bits on your watch until you had a final time for the full 2.5-mile course. Hence - race simulation fartlek.

After a warm-down we hit the Jewish deli across the street on the downhill side of Riverdale and Manhattan College perched on the peak above Jacobus Van Cortlandt's plantation.

The sunny, warm summer afternoon started to yield to the cool of sunset and we drove home to the Jersey side, sure we were getting ready but never underestimating the competition.

# The Church of the Sunday 20-miler

# 18

> "Success is no accident. It is hard work, perseverance, learning, studying, sacrifice and most of all, love of what you are doing or learning to do."
>
> - Pelé

The winter course finished up over Roebling Road to Mountain Top and back down Mine Mount Road so it was more like 21. The summer course crossed the golf course—or more precisely, it wound around the perimeter of the property up all the way around back to Mine Mount, but if there was snow, like today, we had to go up and around on Roebling to Mountain Top and down Post, Mine Mount and back to the high school.

If you have a mind for history or architecture, you may recognize "Roebling." The road was named after the family that designed and built the Brooklyn Bridge. John Augustus Roebling designed the span. His son, civil engineer Washington Roebling contracted caisson disease (the bends) under one of the stone towers when he was overseeing construction. His wife, mostly in secret, took over management of the project to hide the severity of his condition to no celebration of her own. Later, their eccentric grandson Donald invented the LVT amphibious landing craft that would be used on D-Day to land the Allies in France and take Europe back from the Nazis. This is the family the road was named after.

←— —→

My first memory of the 20-course was getting picked up in Mark's White Van at about 12 miles when I was about 12. "The Meat Wagon" was where we ended up if the full course was too much.

But one winter day, I set out with JP to tackle the whole thing. It was cold and in the days before spandex, we wore cotton long johns under our shorts. Turtle necks and knit hats and painters gloves inspired by Boston Billy and we were ready to tackle the world.

The first three miles took us downhill from the high school out Childs Road to Hardscrabble near Rt. 202. From there, we headed up toward Tim Scherman's family's house on the lake. Then up and over into Mendham and a right onto Pleasant Valley Road past the back of Roxiticus Country Club.

It all sounds very simple, but the up and down in elevation of just this part of the course was... significant.

JP told me about the first water stop along the way. An old cistern from one of the ancient estates a few steps into the woods by the bridge at about eight miles. You'd turn left onto the dirt road there to get onto the Jackie-O course.

Yes, THAT Jackie-O, who established residency on Stephens Lane in Bernardsville after it all. It's where Little John and Caroline rode their horses when they were out of the city. I always imagined a secret service detail behind bullet-proof windows as I ran by the house on the trails. I wasn't sure it was THAT house. But I was sure, y'know?

After sucking down some crystal clear water—looking back, the places we took water over the years should have made us much sicker, but that which does not kill us...

We started up the hills where it changed names to Mosle Road and I noticed the wet on my left knee. I leaned against the well to get my balance at the water stop and in a few minutes, it froze the fabric into a dome cover over my knee cap that would remain until we got back indoors.

Over the hill, the surface changed to dirt road and we picked up a black dog. Clearly a mutt. Clearly in need of exercise because he followed us all the way to The Stable in Gladstone.

The Stable for Thoroughbred Motorcars had two locations then. The first was a renovated barn in Gladstone where Mosle Road met Main Street. Dozens of collectible cars, Ferrari to Bentley, sat on this property. The showroom was inside a massive glass window in town where I remember falling in love with a 1936 cream-colored Rolls Royce convertible that could have driven there right out of West Egg.

The course ran down Main Street and turned left on Willow Avenue toward Ravine Lake.

JP told me stories the whole way about the other guys on the team. Places he'd been and run. Key points about the course. He was a year ahead of me and had one 20-miler under his belt already so he was my teacher, my mentor, as well as my friend. I so wanted to have success and know what it felt to finish my 20.

Ravine Lake marks the most amazing, impressive and difficult part of the course. Blairsden looking down on you from its perch above the lake is beautiful. Almost sinister. Just a roof line and seven chimneys show above the canopy of the trees, even in winter.

The Lake Club is right there on the edge of the water. But private enough to not even try for their rest room—even in the off-season. The narrow road, almost a single lane in places wanders along the edge of the lake to the dam at the low end. Rising and falling gently in the shade, you get fooled into believing the course is getting faster. Then you start turning left and up. Up away from the lake. Up and left from 15 to 16-and-a-half miles. Up the old seven-bump carriage road we called Jacob's Ladder where we'd leave water-filled frozen milk bottles in the summertime to have a break and a clean water stop.

Then JP and I hit the flat for a brief tease and left and up Roebling Road—the toughest hill on the course for my money—to Mountain Top. Down Post to Mine Mount Road past Somerset Hills Country Club and back home to sit on the wall in the cold, refreshing air. Never so tired before in my life. But we would get to write 21 miles in our log books that day. My first time. Some of the best of so many miles with JP.

This stretch between 15 and 16-and-a-half is where I learned the power of the 20-miler. After my first 20. The next summer. I was working up to my next 20 and Mark picked me up on the short side of Ravine Lake. About 12 miles. I rode along with him and a few others catching up to the guys training for the '82 cross-country season. It was hot as blazes and they were getting water wherever they could. I watched John Carlotti drive his legs up from the lake to make the left up the hill toward Jacob's Ladder. He stopped briefly to take water. Blanchet caught up just at that time. Then Nielsen and a few of the others. Then a few minutes behind, Larry Sullivan comes hammering up the hill just like the varsity guys bare-chested wearing a pair of white, cotton gym shorts from—what year? But he took water and headed up the hill toward Jacobs like everybody else. We watched them drive their bodies up and over toward St. John's on the Mountain and the back trail onto the golf course property. And I was a convert. This was the workout. This was the time on the road that made all the difference and you could see it shape these runners right in front of your eyes. It was the reason Carlotti dropped almost a minute at Holmdel come November. It was everything Arthur said it was. And each of us has his and her own story of worshipping in the Church of the Sunday 20-miler.

# The Corp. Challenge

# 19

*"Has someone taken your faith
It's real, the pain you feel
Your trust, you must confess
Is someone getting the best, the best, the best
The best of you?"*

- Foo Fighters

**FALL 2005. CENTRAL PARK, MANHATTAN.**

I was less than a half mile from the finish when I felt it. A pronounced "click" in my left foot. If it wasn't so god-awful painful, I think I could tell you if I heard it, too. I started limp-skipping up the right edge of the road inside the mostly dark Central Park alongside thousands of other part-time, older, excessively competitive, has-been, weekend warriors.

I don't know how many others of us running the Chase Corporate Challenge were injured seriously that night in 2005, but I'm fairly certain I was not the only one. The Corporate Challenge is a race—or series of races around the country, really, that encourages corporations to put teams together and go out and run competitively, or semi-competitively together a few times a year. It's an effective team-building event on one hand, and an exercise in risk management for us adult, workaday, weekend athletes on the other. Those of us who still think we can run like our teenage selves.

And because runners are an inherently deranged tribe my first instinct was "let me just finish this race and then figure out what's wrong."

"What the hell happened?" my friend, Harley, asked me when we hooked up after. He was surprised when he came up on me near the finish. Tremendously athletic himself as a cyclist and former Olympic development modern pentathlete, he still didn't think he'd ever outrun me. I wasn't so sure before, but after I felt my foot give way, I was done—but good.

I immediately understood it was a big problem. But couldn't believe it was related. I mean, how could this possibly be related to an injury from two decades before?

I skipped celebratory drinks with my colleagues and subwayed myself downtown to Penn Station, jumped aboard a near-empty NJ Transit car and eventually made my way home.

The next day, I found a sports medicine specialist in Chelsea—he got me doing PT right away—and I practically fell for Jill Butensky the moment she said hello. I fell in love often in those days. My single days. Sometimes several times a day.

I wanted to be a sports medicine specialist when I was a kid. After Tony Sandoval won the 1980 Olympic Trials Marathon and I read about him training to be a sports med doc. They call them physiatrists today. I guess in the end, I didn't have the math, or the science in me.

Several x-rays, palpations, and appointments later, with no improvement and still no diagnosis, Jill came to my rescue again and introduced me to Ethan Ciment, MD. Exceptional surgeon. First time I ever had a doctor younger than me. We hit it off immediately after I told him my Irish Catholic mother wanted more than anything in her life to be a Jewish mother and he would make her proud. Seriously, though, Ethan was and remains one of the best humans I've ever met in my life and a good friend, if separated by time and distance.

I kept up my PT and though he suspected he knew the problem—visions of Dr. Leach dancing in my head—Ethan still hadn't confirmed it. Several weeks later, after he and his partner, who was his partner, acquired their first fluoroscope machine, a kind of live x-ray. If you're not familiar, imagine Buggs Bunny walking behind the x-ray screen and dancing and waving as a live-action skeleton on the move. It wasn't until he could move my foot AND take a gander at the bones inside that he was able to see it. And even then, he could barely see it. But there it was. An impossibly tight seam where there should not be one. The navicular—a tiny bone linking my left ankle to my foot had broken out a new joint. Twenty years after a misdiagnosed, mistreated, stress fracture that never healed, this little bone that had caused consistent pain and discomfort—that had retaught me how to walk with a flipper action on the left side—roll on the right—sharp heel thump on the left. I never knew any different so I didn't understand how wrong it all was. Then one night in Central Park, running with and against my co-workers—CLICK! Broken clean through causing intense, cartilage free, artificial joint pain.

A plan was developed. Surgery scheduled. He'd basically sand or grind the space between the bones to get "good bleeding," then a planned pin, a screw to be put in to help anchor the bone together and allow it to heal itself—finally. The good bleeding would be like using wood glue on a planed joint in a piece of fine furniture. The new, repaired joint would be stronger than the original bone and would never break in that spot again.

"How would you have handled this if you saw me twenty years ago?" I asked my new best friend, Ethan.

"Probably would have just put a couple of screws in," he said.

"And that would have been it?"

"Yep."

I was wheeled into the O.R. where I met up with Ethan and his team. He looked at the Sharpie "yes" and "NO!" written on my two feet and laughed, knowing it was required, but also that some doctors in some places have made mistakes.

"Left foot, right?" he said, smiling.

"Right. It's the left foot," I said feeling not so funny.

Then a tremendously warm whoooooooosh went through my arm into my body.

"Whoa!!!" I said.

"I'm sorry, hun, that was me," the anesthesiologist said leaning in laughing softly behind my head.

Then Ethan told me to count backward from 100.

100... 99... 98... and that was it. I was out.

I have a vague recollection of the two docs discussing two screws and wanting to say, "wait a minute! You said one screw!"

"You heard that?" he asked me later. "Yeah. I heard that."

"That's unusual."

I wore a splint kind of cast for awhile after surgery. Got nauseous on the car ride home. It was either the anesthesia or my mom's driving. The pain was awful. The pain medication just gave me an upset stomach, so none of those opioids for me. I was switched into a cam-walker about a week later. Sort of a boot, walking cast. And eventually transitioned back to physical therapy.

Months and months of PT. Knee problem from compensating for so long. Adjustment and trying to get movement back into my broken foot. Blinding pain from muscles and soft tissue that hadn't moved that way in so long.

Over time, the pain subsided and I was able to walk, then jog a little bit. Then I had a great idea. How about a marathon?

I started training and worked up to about 30 miles a week at one point. Then about a month before the Space Coast Marathon, my achilles flared up. And didn't let me even give it a go.

I had another idea. How about an attempt at the mile record for 45-year-olds? Get back to training. Then after a few months, the achilles. Then Trautmann shows up on social media running 4:16 indoors. Great run by that guy again.

So here I am. Years later. I can still predict the rain. I still can't run the way I want to. I still look at all the people running around my neighborhood and on the trails near me and think, "howcum they can run without pain and I can't?"

Yet, I keep trying. Keep the hope. Keep the faith that one day, I'll have a run to remember again. I sometimes think about the Bryn Mawr docs and wonder if they can run. If they're in pain. If they're still around. Or retired. Or beyond retired. I think about so many of the people I knew at Villanova who thought they knew what was going on and judged when they looked my way. And I know they have no concept of what really happened. And probably never will. Maybe it's better that way.

But no matter. There are more things to do.

←  →

## SEPTEMBER 26, 2024

I spent about a half an hour or more on the phone this morning talking to a man I haven't spoken to since about 1988. Thirty-six years. Dr. Gary Gordon retired about five years ago as one of the top orthopedic and sports medicine specialists in the region, if not the country. I met him at one of the darkest moments of my life. I was dejected, defeated, a little lost, unable to see where life would take me. And totally alone. I was sure no one understood what I was going through. But he and his staff enabled me to smile. I walked into his office, through the waiting area and there were enormous windows looking out on a stadium I'd only seen from the other side. There were exam and treatment tables and tools of his trade all across the floor and an absolutely panoramic view of the castle that is Franklin Field. They welcomed me. There were several other athletes there going through all sorts of exercises and grimacing in effort. One was a football player I recognized from Villanova. They were taking off the cast that encased his left leg and knee since his surgery. I watched as the motorized blade vibrated through the cast and they exposed his leg to the light for the first time in so long. So many stitches itching to be removed. It looked thin, and wrinkled, and weak compared to his right leg. But he couldn't wait to get going on his rehab. The staff of PTs and some student trainers were all incredibly welcoming, positive, and joking. It was the first time in a very long time I remember feeling sunny. I don't know that it changed any of the facts for me. Or results. But it made a difference and to this day, I'm grateful.

Because I remembered his name, I looked up Dr. Gordon and found his old practice with a lovely little farewell message to his patients on the website. I called the office and they graciously offered to take a message for him. Protective of him, as they should be, in case I was some kind of a nut.

He told me he likes to call back the runners. I don't really know if he remembered me, specifically, but he made me feel like he did. Or started to. I told him why I was calling and what I was trying to remember. I went to another doc at Penn, but couldn't remember his name.

"Torg," he said.

"What?"

"Joe Torg."

"How do you spell that?"

And I looked up Dr. Joseph Torg on my computer right then and there and recognized his photo immediately.

"That's him."

And I went over my story. And told him about the bone scan. And how encouraged I felt walking into his bright, beautiful office on the Penn campus.

And he told me a story I'd never heard before.

When he started at Penn in about 1978, he remembered one athlete came in with foot pain keeping him from playing football. A pro athlete. They eventually landed almost by accident on a diagnosis of a navicular stress fracture. The bone is so small and has such poor blood flow, it was difficult to see and heal and even diagnose. The pain tended to be "vague" and "referred" to other parts of the foot and leg. This sounded familiar to me. The MRI wasn't available in those days and a bone scan required a special camera that Penn did not have at the time. So they sent him to the Hospital for Special Surgeries in New York City where he met Dr. Helene Pavlov, a radiologist who eventually wrote a book called "The Running Athlete" with Dr. Torg. In the end, he said, they identified the fracture. Did surgery, putting in a couple of screws, and the footballer went on to play again.

That was the only navicular stress fracture they had that year.

Over the next year, they treated thirteen more of them.

It's not that there were that many more, they just got better at identifying and treating them. And those numbers kept going up. Usually male, tall, athletes who ran a lot in their sports. Cornering and lateral movement of basketball and football players especially.

So when I showed up in 1987 complaining of the same pain. The same issues. And went to Bryn Mawr Orthopedic Associates, who were not really sports medicine specialists, it shouldn't have been surprising they had no idea what they were dealing with. Dr. Gordon, like his tribe, was not one to blame another doc and wouldn't say directly that this was the source of my real problem, but clearly, it was a problem in the profession. If I'd seen him as a college or high school athlete in 1975, even the experts wouldn't have known what to do. They wouldn't have been able to see it. In 1987, they were making strides. And publishing. And the real docs in the sports specialty knew what was happening. It took a ton of work, and research and study. The docs only claiming the specialty as a marketing tool still did not know. It's the magical thinking again. You can't just claim expertise you haven't worked for.

Thanks to Dr. Gordon, I found several papers almost right away as well as a used copy of "The Running Athlete" by Drs. Pavlov and Torg for $150 on Amazon.

I read the abstracts of the papers published in 1981, and 1985, and 1990 and it felt like I could be reading my own journal. The description of the pain and the experience was as close to an exact match as I could imagine.

It was good talking to Dr. Gordon. The feeling I got from the retired doc was the same feeling I got from him when he was practicing. Joyful and welcoming. Helpful and generous. We talked a little bit about running history and his role as volunteer at the Penn Relays. We lamented the cancellation of the meet during the pandemic and both had wonderful things to say about Dave Johnson, the meet director. I thanked him and said goodbye. I don't know if I'll ever get in touch with him again, but I remain grateful for knowing him.

So in the end, it seems Bryn Mawr Orthopedic Associates was only masquerading as a sports medicine clinic when they landed their Villanova contract. When they didn't have the expertise or curiosity to be that. To claim to be that. They were non-experts claiming to be experts. And they hurt people as a result. I know I wasn't the only one.

I know this kind of charlatanism is not rare in America. Sometimes, it's not even malicious. But most businesses don't actively cause harm just because of their hubris. Some people really think that if they are sports fans and former athletes AND doctors, they can call themselves physiatrists or sport medicine specialists.

Eventually, Jill the PT introduced me to Ethan at Chelsea Foot & Ankle and that was good for me. Ethan thought differently about his profession. And it made him better. The best, for me.

But it all takes time to find these better people. And when you're taught to place your trust in people pretending they're more of an expert than they are, it really takes time. And the patient suffers. I can only imagine how I'd feel if it was a more severe condition. Not a sports injury. Something life-threatening. There are incompetent people in every profession, but in some fields, it matters more than others. The stakes are higher and we should not allow these sorts of reputational fictions to exist.

After the surgery was scheduled, Jill asked if she could come to observe.

"You mean, in the operating room?" I asked.

She nodded. Smiling.

"Sure. Why not?" I said after a quick consider.

I asked if she'd talked to Ethan, and she said he told her if I said it was ok, it would be ok with him. So I said... ok.

A few weeks after the surgery, I was feeling some pain at the incision site. When I was working with Jill, I said I wondered if one of the screws was working its way out and she laughed hysterically.

"What?"

"If you saw the how hard he worked to get that screw in there, you wouldn't be asking that question," she said.

I pictured him all dressed for surgery with a Craftsman screwdriver in his hand using his whole body to countersink the screw. I called Ethan a "great surgeon" once and he told me no, "I'm more of a carpenter." It is hard not to love Ethan. I could have used a more aggressive carpenter in 1988.

In the end, what I think happened was, I had a stress fracture that over time and misdiagnosis and continued training broke through partially. And because of the equipment, treatment methods and knowledge of the time, even when I did get to the right docs, they couldn't see the severity of it. So they assumed six weeks in a non-weight bearing cast would heal it. But it didn't. And eventually, after almost two decades of walking and running and standing and exercising, the little navicular bone that could, couldn't anymore and broke clean through. And that was painful. In more than one way. And I still have pain. Not every day, but almost every day. And I can still tell you when it's going to rain.

People sometimes ask me if I sued them. The docs? Villanova? Or why I didn't. I sometimes think I should have. I'm pretty sure I had plenty of evidence for a case. I found a letter my dad sent that I'd never seen. He made it clear that there was a case. That explains the change in Dan, the arrogant mustachioed trainer. One day out of the blue, he became extremely friendly. Which was weird. And maybe more unpleasant than it was before.

# The Pie Run

## 20

*"And even if we are occupied by most important things, if we attain to honor, or fall into great misfortune—still let us remember how good it was once here, when we were all together, united by a good and kind feeling which made us better perhaps than we are."*

- Fyodor Dostoevsky

Turn up at The Polo Grounds any Thanksgiving Day morning at about 8:30 a.m. and you will be welcomed by a group of anywhere from a couple of dozen to fifty or so Bernards High School, and MMRD alumni, family, friends, and generally just welcoming people. It's one of the longest-standing traditions in our tribe.

Announcement and invitation not required. I remember being at the first, but I don't remember exactly how many there have been.

Run and supported by the Sullivans—Larry's wife Maureen, son John, and daughter Megan McDowell. How it goes is this:

Everybody drives up the pool road and parks at the edge of the fields.

When enough people are there to have a conversational quorum, we get out of the cars and start reconnecting. It's just another event where I met so many people I didn't know well before who were connected to the

Long Red Line in one way or another. I never knew John Sullivan that well, but we talk like old friends. Everyone from the 1970s classes like Tommy Lewis and Ed Johnson. I've run there with Brian and Sarah Bomberger. Some of the current team is almost always there. And kids of the alumni. Not all runners, but all Bernards-connected people happy to meet up and remember things.

The "race" is not so much a race as a prediction contest. Rain or shine, write down a time you think you can run for the course. Or a time you can predict yourself running away for awhile and coming back. Walk if you want. The only rule, no watches. You can't keep track, you have to do it naturally. Best guess.

Whoever comes closest to their predicted time wins a pie.

Whoever came from the longest distance wins a pie.

The youngest or oldest wins a pie - or something else.

The prizes can be a little random. But the celebration is warm and joyful.

And everyone is invited back to the Sullivan-McDowell home on Old Army Road for breakfast after. Megan and her husband bought her childhood home a few years ago. So much continuity on Thanksgiving day. All shoes left in the front hallway. Bagels and coffee provided.

All Bernardsville runners and friends of Bernardsville runners are welcome to this homecoming of sorts at the old, original Bernards High cross-country course.

To bring all of this full-circle, we should pay a little attention to one week in 2005. Not exclusively tied to the Pie Run here, but again, in the interest of harmony and continuity, Ed Mather passed away on June 12, 2005 at the age of 75. In his obituary on the front page of the Bernardsville News, his old friend Larry Sullivan was quoted.

"He created an almost magical atmosphere for these boys," he said. "It was really a way of life, not just school."

I had my differences with Mr. Mather over my time there. A complicated relationship to be sure. But in the end as they say, attention must be paid.

In that most curious of ways the world has of working sometimes, Larry Sullivan passed away just four days later, on June 16, 2005 at the age of just 72. A retired Air Force Colonel and pilot, a lifelong runner, and a tremendous friend to so may of us, Larry Sullivan was as much a part of the magic of Bernardsville running as any single person.

I remember more than once, him putting a kettle on for tea, then lacing up his shoes for a run only to forget the kettle on the stove. I don't know how many burned out kettles they had to replace over the years, but he had his run in mind and that was what he was going to do. He was just as likely to turn up to practice to get a steady ten miler in with us as he was to turn up at the Bernards Invitational in a seersucker suit and white bucks wearing a straw skimmer from another age.

And the Pie Run is a perfect way to preserve our collective memory of his impact. And even though he never went himself, my dad was always disappointed I didn't bring home a pie.

# Takanassee. Gesundheit.

# 21

"Show a little faith, there's magic in the night."
- Thunder Road

A couple of times a year in the midst of summer training, the MMRD crowd would pile into our cars and head south on Rt. 287 to the Garden State Parkway, pay the tolls past Holmdel to exit 105 and travel east along sandy Rt. 36 into Long Branch. There was a pier with games and a haunted house, boardwalk food and the Atlantic Ocean lapping up on the sand. And there was a small inlet by St. Michael's Catholic Church that fed into Lake Takanassee. "Tak," we all called it. It's all still there minus the pier and the haunted house that was destroyed by a suspicious fire in June of 1987.

Sunday was our long run. Sometimes a hard run, too. But always long. Mark called it The Church of the Sunday 20-miler. We'd often go out on Sunday afternoons for an easy short morning or maybe as much as the five miles of Phizer-Ballantine if we felt frisky to shake out the legs for the week to come. Three to six miles to round out mileage for the week. The counting of miles ended on Sunday night and there was always a little time left to get to the round number. Turn double digits into triple digits.

Then, maybe twice a summer, we'd get our bright yellow singlets out of mothballs and toe the line at Tak.

Founded by the famed Shore AC in 1964, the Lake Takanassee Series is one of the longest-running road race series in the region—maybe in the country. It's still there and still running, every Monday night through the summer, a gaggle of road runners turn out to the parking lot behind St. Michael's on Ocean Avenue for a chance to race four laps around the lake. 5,000m. 5k. 3.1 miles. In the summer heat.

Regulars amass points for performances over the series and compete Winston Cup-style for a season champion title.

Today, the organization and signups are all digitized like everything else, everywhere else. In the 80s, there was a club mom at a card table taking $5 and $10 dollar bills into a metal cash box and handing out 3 x 5 cards and safety pins for race numbers. I can only imagine what it was like in 1964, '65, '66.

The MMRD crowd would descend on the shore like a pack—the same way we did most places. Polite, but impossible to ignore. Junior high schoolers to adults, but the high schoolers made the biggest impression—varsity, fit, fast, and vocal.

A casual atmosphere, but we were there for a reason. A test. An unrested time trial of sorts designed to pick up the leg turnover for the first time and put a clock to it. To see what kind of shape we were in and to compare July to August and have a better understanding of fitness as we approached the racing season.

Plus a nice getaway to the beach and the old Long Branch boardwalk for an evening. Windmill hot dogs and the smell of salt lingered in the car as we made our way back home to our inland mountain town.

20 miles on Sunday.

5k time trial down the shore on Monday.

We can rest on Tuesday twice this summer.

Mark called it Camp Pain for a reason.

# The Boilermaker

# 22

*"What're you talking about? We've got one heavily armed recreational vehicle here, man."*

- Private John Winger

Utica, New York, is a city of about 65,000 souls lying west of the state capital of Albany, east of Syracuse, where they invented cold, and about a four-hour chartered Kent bus ride from the Bernardsville train station.

A working city along the Mohawk River and Erie canal complex, the city grew as a part of the industrial age and dipped into recession as other methods of shipping developed.

In 1978, in the midst of the first American Running Boom, The Boilermaker Race was founded as the unofficial 15k US Championship. That first race was won by Rick Rojas of Boulder, Colorado, in 45:38 by almost three minutes.

In the summer of 1980, two years later, Mark Wetmore brought a team of Mine Mount Road Department runners to take part for the first time. We traveled upstate by charter bus, stayed in the local Sheraton, went for a run around the city to shake out our legs, carbo-loaded at the race's official pre-race spaghetti dinner, then at 7:30 a.m. the next morning, 30 of us in every age group disembarked to the start line and took the day by storm.

Taking a trip away from home when you're 12 or 13 is an exciting proposition. Saying goodbye to dad and climbing aboard the bus—even just a 4-hour ride to upstate New York is an exotic, frightening journey at that age. JP made fun of my musical choice I was listening to on a Panasonic mono tape recorder through a single ear phone—the Walkman wasn't widely available in Sony-land yet and Apple was just a box in a Palo Alto garage. There were boom boxes on laps and large, can earphones plugged in to take the edge off the trip.

I think I was the youngest there, but we had every age group represented for men and women on that bus. I remember everyone being excited to race that odd 9.3-mile distance on the roads of Oneida County.

The batch of us broke into age-appropriate conversation groups on the bus, but the older folks looked after us youngsters. Talked to us like regular people, not just kids. It's how we learned to travel. How to act. How to tip. How to say "hello" and "thank you." And be grateful for other people.

Somewhere along the early part of the ride, the bus coughed and smoked and drifted off to the side of the highway. And we waited and waited for a replacement Kent Bus to come to our rescue. Again, the days before cell phones and I was sitting near the front where the driver was calling his dispatcher for help on a CB radio.

When the replacement arrived, we spilled out of the first bus with our gear, reloaded the storage bins of the new one, and climbed aboard again for the rest of the ride north to Utica. It may as well have been Oz to me.

When we pulled into the Sheraton, the four-hour trip had turned into five and a half. Maybe six. The hotel seemed like the Savoy to me and we were called down to the lobby in an hour for a group run to shake out the bus ride.

The city was alive with activity. We ran up the sidewalks of the business district together. Jim Smith of Haddonfield was up at the front with Mark who'd committed a route to memory. Jim Smith, no relation, was with us. He was the All-Groups cross-country champ from '79 and now at Stanford. Another one who might as well have been Babe Ruth to me, he was always "Jim Smith of Haddonfield," or "Jim Smith." Never just Jim. Buck Logan and Pete Carroll ran along with high schoolers Stogryn and Flood and Blanchet. I was toward the back with Hallinan who made me feel like a little brother.

We ran in a sidewalk column two and three abreast apologizing to the other pedestrians looking on this crowd of disciplined weirdo joggers running through their town. They looked at us as if we were aliens. We weren't the only group in town for the race—the field was about 1,100 or more runners—but we were probably one of the biggest. And we moved together.

As we trotted up through a sidewalk art show, someone—maybe Hallinan, maybe Blanchet, got us shouting the cadence from Stripes a la Bill Murray.

"Boom chaka laka laka, boom chaka laka laka, boom chaka laka laka, boom..."

The movie had just come out. And it made me laugh—and excited to be a part of the group. "Stripes" starring Bill Murray and Harold Ramis. 1980. Ivan Reitman, director.

We finished our run, showered and dressed back at the hotel and reboarded the bus bound for our spaghetti dinner. Our large group was recognized by the M.C. Made sufficient fun of, and then we ate. Then we slept. Then we got up and tumbled out of the bus at the start where we, as a group, took a large number of the age-group trophies. Paul Revere silver bowls that got filled over and over again at the sponsor and finish line site, the Utica West End Brewery. It was a joyous ride home. For the adults especially.

## WORKOUT: Prepping for States

Freshman year was a bit of an all-comers experience for me. I'd trained hard all summer and was ready to make the varsity seven, I thought.

Cross-country is a team sport unlike anything else. You have a team of people running an individual sport. They don't pass a ball or a puck. They don't tag each other out like tag-team wrestling or a relay. They each run their own races. All together. Maybe 300 or so runners in a championship race. Over turf and hills and mud and wind. So even your time over 5,000m doesn't matter all that much.

Each person scores the same number of points as his or her place in the race. First place equals one point. Fiftieth place equals fifty points. So the team with the lowest score wins. Generally, the top five runners score and the remaining two (seven on a team) put additional places between their team and the next team.

So if a team places first through fifth, they score 15 points. If they place the first seven places, the next team can score eight through twelfth places. Or 50 points. 15-50 is a perfect score.

In larger meets, it is much more complicated.

To make a competitive cross-country team's top seven as a freshman is a happy accomplishment. It turned out, we had eight very good guys. So I was fifth through eight man on any given day of the season, not guaranteed a spot on the state championship team or any other meet.

I ran fifth man in the University of Virginia invitational early in the season. And was called eighth man just before the NJ State All-Groups. So I ran the TAC Jr. Olympics instead. Then some indoor running, mostly at two-miles. Then, as spring turned around, I ran a very competitive mile at the Bernards Invitational, but as the state championship loomed, the only open slot for me and senior Mike Hinman on this team was in the 800m. As a result, our training shifted. Shorter repeats. Faster. Under 60-second laps all the time.

To be prepared to race well at every distance from 5,000m cross-country to 800m on the track in the spring to the 3,000m steeplechase in the summer is a strange and complicated assignment that required real specificity training leading up to each different distance. With all the distance training, the strength was certainly there. We just needed to polish the speed.

⇇ ⇉

The Ladder:
Multiple ladder workouts were the assignment of the day.
2 x 600m @ 1:30
2 x 400m @ :60
4 x 200m @ :30 or faster with limited recovery.

And Mike and I both made it into the Group I 800m. We both ran under 2:00 minutes. And we both watched John Carlotti run away from us.

## Ever-evolving

# 23

"From enjoyment comes the will to win."
- Arthur Lydiard

For those in need of understanding. The Wetmore method began in the roots of the Lydiard method. Mark met Arthur Lydiard who famously trained Peter Snell, Murray Halberg, and Barry Magee of New Zealand to Olympic glory. Learned from him. And eventually asked the coach about training young people and new runners, specifically. Lydiard didn't have anything specific at the time even though he understood there was a difference in what they needed and the way they developed.

Wetmore took what he learned, then applied it and tested it and changed it. Adapted it. The early days—my early days—what we were doing looked a lot like something out of *Running, the Lydiard Way*.

But it changed all the time. Never stopped changing.

The challenges we faced were unique to each of us. The questions different and specific: How do you peak at different, multiple times a year? How do you stay prepared for three seasons - and stay fast. Maybe even get faster over time and sometimes with a need to do it more than once per year. Penn in April - States in June. Unknown other opportunities.

The answer lies in the preparation. The method was long distance. Long, fast, distance. And consistency. Commitment. Every day. Rest when needed, but every day. Big base training in the summer yielding to hill and strength training yielding to eventual specificity training to polish speed for specific events. Always with the long run at the center of everything. The two-hour Sunday run. The Church of the Sunday 20-Miler. Build the base strength. The engine of everything else. How else does a runner like Peter Snell win the Olympic 800m? Training like a marathoner. The best cars are built for Le Mans, not Raceway Park.

A common question now is... Would today's parents allow it? Truth? My answer, I'm not sure parents of that time would allow it, either, if they really knew. Other than ours. Because there was trust.

In the end, I could walk you through it all. All the workouts. The times. The assignments. The courses. The hills. I could get intensely specific. But it wouldn't give you what you need. There's something else. And that's what they're talking about when they ask what is the Wetmore factor? What makes the difference? I lived it, and I'm not sure I could explain it to you exactly.

# WORKOUT: Mt. Kilamanjaro

Another trail in our repertoire was known by the same name as the Hemingway story. Without the snow. Mt. Kilamanjaro was an entrance to the trails near Jockey Hollow Road and Hardscrabble. A short jog into the woods there dropped us at a flat straightaway that might have been an estate drive back 100 years ago. The house, though, was long gone. Follow the straightway for a few meters and the trail began to rise. Not steep. Just steady.

Then it hairpinned to the left and went up. Then hairpinned to the right and then up. And at the very top of the hill, the trail curled around to the left once more and that was it. The better part of 600m up the hill. Steady, not steep.

And we would do hard pickups up the hill. Fast and hard, but not completely sprints.

10-12 repeats. As fast as we could manage while avoiding our teammates jogging back down two-abreast.

This was a variation of the same workout we did in the older days on the lengthy portion of Seney Drive, the longest hill on the home cross-country course. All pavement, that was. And no turns. Just one 400m straightaway. Times 12. Another workout we loved and hated in equal measure.

# The Boards

## 24

"Oh to live on Sugar Mountain
With the barkers and the colored balloons
You can't be twenty on Sugar Mountain
Though you're thinking that
you're leaving there too soon
You're leaving there too soon."

- Neil Young

I posted the videos to YouTube so other people could enjoy them. It felt a little self-serving since so much of it was of me, but it was my dad who shot them after all. And they may be some of the only video documentation from that time, so I shared.

I don't go back to look much. Once in awhile. I show Aiden because it's nice to remember and he likes to see what it was like in those days. I wish I had more from my dad's time or other Bernards days, but there are just photos—stills—and clippings from the paper.

Mark drove us down to Villanova one day that winter after I'd gotten my Millrose invitation. Just the two of us. A tough invite to wangle, Millrose. I'd tried for the last two years and came up short to Bill Kolb of CBA last year when he out-kicked me at the the trials in Jadwin. I ended up running faster than him for the year and felt like I should have gotten an invitation, but the Millrose people tended to favor seniors and sometimes New Yorkers.

Disappointment is a funny thing. I had many, many good opportunities and a lot of success. Some earned. Some luck. Some both, because that's how they work together. But it would have been nice to run against those guys a year before and get a little extra experience on that wooden teacup of a track.

The running track at Madison Square Garden used for the better part of a century was built on a wooden frame with a wooden running surface. Originally planks, later some version of plywood decking. Originally unfinished, then painted black to last longer, then finally painted yellow and orange for visibility on television, the oval was 11 laps to the mile and banked to about 22 degrees on the turns with temporary construction so it could be pulled out in the hours after the meet for a basketball game or a circus or a boat show.

The whole track bounced with a full field racing around the turns. It truly felt like running inside a delicate piece of china. 160 yards to the lap compared to 400m outdoors. For reference, today, the NCAA limits the bank to 18 degrees for official competition. The straightaways were as long as they could manage in the space with the four-lane turns fitting inside of what would be the glass of the Rangers' hockey rink. The lap markings were impossible to find if you weren't familiar with the oddball distance and if you were a taller runner, you had to learn how to use the steep banks to your advantage or the shorter runners would use the tight turns to beat you senseless.

'Nova had the old Madison Square Garden track they set up outside to train on. Unknown how they got it, but there it was. Someone had graciously shoveled the snow off the board track. And we had permission from someone to use the track. I think.

I warmed up running around a campus I wouldn't come to know until later. But it was exciting to see the place. The little road that wound itself around by the library and the big, gray stone buildings that could be classrooms or chapels. I ran around the modern buildings and found my way back to the boards where Mark was waiting for me.

I laced up my spikes after jogging a few laps on the banks to get used to the shape and size of the oval.

The color and lane lines had worn off the wooden surface and I could see the splinters. But it was new to me and fun, and I couldn't begin to know what to expect.

The workout was a variation of a ladder and at 11 laps to the mile, I never really knew where I was in the 200-400-600 I was doing.

The experience mattered more than the effort that day. And bore little resemblance to what it would feel like in the Garden in a few weeks.

Cold. Tights. Long sleeves. Running fast in spikes.

After working out, we took a drive down into Philly. Mark had to visit the city library for some reason. I'd changed into dry clothes and we had a bite to eat along the way, but we drove past the Art Museum where Rocky ran up the stairs and down the broad Ben Franklin Parkway up to the front of the library building. Huge and white stone that looked like it should be in Washington DC.

I wandered the stacks until Mark found what he was looking for and finished his project. Then we piled back in the car parked along the street and headed the 100 miles back to Bernardsville listening to music the whole way. Neil Young. The Stones. Songs with stories. Nothing too contemporary.

It wasn't the first or only time I spent a full day alone with Mark. I sometimes wonder what would have happened if I said I wanted him to come to Villanova with me. If they'd bring him on as a coach. If he'd fit. If he wanted to. How would it have been different for the both of us? If it would have even been possible. The university, like the church, liked to keep things in the family.

Sitting in the grass at Holmdel Park one day in the sun years later, I was waiting with Mark for one of the state championship races to come storming up the starting hill. I don't remember everything we talked about, but he did ask me if I had any regrets. I told him no. But I was lying.

So often, I work to think things better than they are. I don't think that's completely a bad thing. I don't like concentrating on the worst possibilities. It makes me overwhelmed. And lowers my expectations of the world around me when I want to have a high opinion of those things. Besides, I like to believe things can turn around. In a big way. Very quickly. I've seen it happen. I can't stop believing in that.

But to this day I wish I'd told him the truth.

Maybe I just wasn't sure of my whole story at that time. Maybe that's why it's taken so long to write this down.

Yes. Of course I have regrets. I regret I never ran as fast as I wanted to. I regret I never embraced the time part of racing as much as the racing part of racing. I might be in some record books today. I regret I didn't train hard enough that summer before I started my first college season. For a long time, I thought that I ruined my life with that summer job and that lack of focus. I regret I never ran an outdoor track race in a Villanova singlet. I regret I didn't consider other schools in the first place. I regret I didn't push back on those Bryn Mawr doctors and their lack of diagnoses at the time. After all, I knew as much or more than they did about what I was feeling. Why wouldn't my assessment be as valid as theirs? Just because they had alphabet soup after their names? I regret not being stronger with Jenks about red-shirting and taking charge of my own destiny more. I regret letting myself get so depressed by it all it distracted me from what I was there for. I regret I enjoyed being alone so much I didn't spend as much time as I should have with my friends. I regret I didn't move farther away from home when I had the chance and embrace the adventure of life. I regret I thought there would always be time.

It's taken me a very long time to recognize all those things that I tucked away inside my chest didn't really belong to me at all. Inside my chest, y'know, where the heart is. I was just a kid. And I was really hurt. And it wasn't my fault. And I wasn't trying to get away with anything. My world got turned upside down at a time in life when the idea of shifting directions is very, very difficult. At least it was for me. It took me a very long time to figure out something else I was good at. Something I liked doing. That could have a positive impact on people and the world.

Do I still wrestle with that feeling of regret and missed opportunity? I wouldn't be human if I didn't. But I'm better at it than I ever was. Having Heather in my life and the pair of us bringing Aiden into the world brought all of that into much sharper relief for me. I'm a writer and a communicator and I've helped clients and customers and colleagues and friends and family with all of that. And that has made me feel important in the world in some way. Being a dad to my son is what makes me feel most important in the world. Because if I'm 100 percent about anything, I'm 100 percent sure he will be a good influence on his world. And that makes me feel satisfied.

It was supposed to be happy ultrasound day. Heather was at about 20 weeks and my parents came to Riverview Hospital with us for her checkup. We listened to his very strong heartbeat first, which always made us happy. And as we watched the screen, we joked how he liked to hold his hands up in front of his face in utero playing hide and seek with the camera.

It was Heather who noticed it first.

"Wait! Go back," she told the technician.

He'd moved his hands away for a moment.

"Is that a cleft palate on the left side?"

Stunned quiet and clearly afraid to give her own opinion, the tech said, "You can see that?"

Heather, of course, as a highly trained medical professional and acupuncturist with multiple advanced degrees was trained to read just about any radiological scan. So, yes, she could see it. I was blind.

"Let me get the doctor."

And we waited.

The doctor explained what we were seeing. What Heather had already understood. And we were taken into a very small office of another doctor. A supervisor of some kind who gave us what I've come to call the fear of God speech. All the things a cleft palate could possibly indicate. It could be this chromosomal abnormality or this other chromosomal abnormality. Or it could be this terrible thing or that awful condition or disease. It could be fatal. It could be lifelong treatment of something horrific and expensive. "And you have choices."

"Or it could be just a rogue cleft?" Heather asked.

The doctor nodded.

"Yes, it could be just a cleft."

[Long pause.]

Maybe the longest my mother had kept her mouth shut at one time, ever.

"You listen to me," Heather said looking this doctor in the eyes. "If you EVER talk to me about 'other options' ever again, I'm walking out of this hospital right to the other OB group down the street and EVERYONE will know why."

And that was the end of the discussion.

Heather is the kindest, sweetest, most generous human being I've ever known. Given my personality, I sometimes find it to be irritating how kind, sweet, and generous she is to some people. But she is also a brilliant, powerful, logical, courageous woman to be messed with only at your own peril.

The next days and weeks were overwhelming. We didn't know what to do or expect. We told my parents right then and there that we didn't want anyone to know until we got our feet under us. We told Heather's mother the same thing. Both of our mothers wanted to tell everyone, everything, all the time. This was not helpful.

We told our friends Jill and Jerry Wichtel who we knew we could trust both to hold our confidence and be helpful. Jill, a former social worker, went into research mode and came back with two thoughts. Children's Hospital of Philadelphia and NYU. She said the only place we should be considering was the NYU Cleft Palate Team and Dr. Court Cutting. Yes, ironic a surgeon would be named "Cutting," but more on that later.

We called both hospitals and waited for a return call.

Shelly Cohen called back from NYU first and the first thing out of her mouth was "congratulations on your new baby boy!" Over a long, caring, informative conversation she made Heather feel like there was a plan. An understanding of what comes next. Shelly ended by reminding her that she was giving birth to a baby boy, not a cleft. And that was the first restful night of sleep since "happy ultrasound day."

We eventually met Dr. Court Cutting, the surgeon, who introduced us to the NYU team method called nasoavicular molding. Developed by he and his partner on the team Dr. Barry Grayson who appeared to be a cross between the most brilliant medical mind you could imagine and Dumbledore in a beautiful, silk, custom-made bow tie. Heather loved him immediately and made him teach her something new every time we met with him. Every week. This made him love her.

The molding therapy used Aiden's natural growth patterns and elasticity to grow the 13.5mm gap he had at birth to zero at the time of his first surgery. Like guiding the growth of a Bonsai tree. A passion of Dr. Grayson, who was also an accomplished painter and sculptor.

The first surgery was seven and a half anxious hours at age four and a half months. Then the second surgery about four and a half hours at just short of a year. The traditional cleft correction process done at most other hospitals involves up to 14 or more surgeries by the time the child is a teenager. The NYU team vision was clearly superior.

Cutting told us one of the main goals of the process beyond getting the best possible correction was to not allow the kids to become perpetual patients. To not feel like sickly kids. Because they aren't. Not at all. I met another dad one day who was talking about his nine-year-old daughter who was back for a follow-up. He said "they're just tougher kids that way. They don't cry about things. They're not bothered by things the way other kids are."

And that's been true. Aiden has grown into a smart, caring, intuitive, kid who isn't afraid of taking on a challenge. He's started running cross country with one of the best school teams in the nation and is working hard to make its way up the line. The cleft repair is so perfect, even we don't notice it anymore. He's not a perpetual patient and has never felt that way. We are grateful to Dr. Cutting and Dr. Grayson and Shelly and the whole team we got to know during this time in his life. And Dr. Christina Carter who we still travel back to New Jersey to see as his specialty orthodontist and dentist, mentor, and friend. She has become family.

Every kid, every family, has their own challenges they need to navigate over the course of their lives. I just feel incredibly fortunate that my folks got me with Dr. Wood and his all-exercise-all-the-time approach when I was a kid. And Heather and I, with the help of our friend, Jill, found the NYU Team and Dr. Grayson especially who guided us through a very difficult year and a half riding the ferry to the east side of Manhattan every week. Such an amazing result. Such a spectacular result. And neither of us needed to feel like a sickly, hospital kid.

# Checkmate

# 25

"Josie's on a vacation far away.
Come around and talk it over.
So many things that I wanna say.
Y'know I like my girls a little bit older..."

- The Outfield

One Sunday after our long run, and lunch, and a nap, Ranjan called me. From just two houses down the street on the other side of the Kulick house. I could see Gypsy chasing a ball around his back yard from my bedroom window.

"I'm going up to Livingston Mall to get a computer game. Wanna come?"

"Oh yeah. What game?"

"Chess," he said.

"Why not just get out a chess board?

[Pause.]

"Wanna come?"

Hitting the mall with Ranjan was an experience. He was always much more interested in image than I was and his style tended toward Naperville five years ago. Members only.

When he arrived in Bernardsville in the last few weeks of our freshman year, he came out to practice wearing white knee socks right up to his patellas. Like James Robinson. Usually with red stripes around his calves. And we made fun of this unmercifully.

The better part of three years later, he'd made the move to short socks, but still favored Bob Seger over Springsteen. He made me look at western boots and always new sunglasses. And Sam Goody was always an adventure. I tended toward Van Halen and loud guitars while he traveled in what would become power pop and what the girls were listening to. INXS. The Fixx. The Outfield. Wham. I probably should have paid more attention to that part of his personality. I might have found it helpful.

"Computer chess? Why don't you just get a chess board?"

"I have a chess board. This is COMPUTER chess!" This was a point we hit several times over and over. A running gag all afternoon.

So we hopped into his family's VW Golf and headed up Rt. 287 to buy a computer chess game at the shop inside Livingston Mall. And walk around. And have a Nathan's hot dog. I always craved hot dogs after a long run. And ride the escalators. And check out the girls we didn't know. And never would.

When we got back, Ranjan went to set up his game and I went home.

"I'll call when I have it working," he said.

A couple of hours later, he called.

"Oh, you got it set up?"

[Long pause.]

"No. I couldn't get it working," he said. "I got a chess board."

That was life with Ranjan.

# Elite - a shoe story

# 26

"Instant gratification takes too long."
- Carrie Fisher

I learned the meaning of the word "elite" from a shoe and a sense of disappointment. I remember graduating to that time where I would race in different shoes than I would train in.

I ran my first race at Van Cortlandt Park in a pair of white Adidas that I loved. Bright and unscarred with a sole full of knobs. With the Adidas version of the Nike waffle sole, the TRX reminded me of the name of my dad's car—the TR6.

I trained in them and raced in them. Didn't wear them to school. Never did that. Running shoes were always for running. And they looked good in pictures.

But then came the time. Racing shoes. Lighter. Faster. Different. Because racing was different than training and I didn't know the names of every model.

I watched Alberto Salazar win the 1980 New York City Marathon in what I thought were the coolest shoes of all time and wanted what would become the "Eagle" so badly.

I asked Mark what shoes I should get and he didn't even hesitate—Nike Elites.

So my dad got me a pair. I couldn't wait to get them. I so wanted spikes, but not yet. And when the guy at the Sneaker Barn in Chester brought out the blue box with that familiar cool swoosh on it, I was done drawing the Adidas trefoil on my notebook covers forever.

He kneeled down in front of me the way we bought shoes in those days and opened the box and there they were. Blue and yellow and brand new with that sneakery rubber smell and they were exactly NOT what I had in my mind.

Shoes and spikes are funny things to a runner. So important in so many ways, but the choices we make are based on so many ridiculous things like color and brand and shape.

My first pair of spikes were a blue Adidas model—the stripes and the "U" that held the laces was made of some hard, immovable plastic with a sawtooth edge that gave me blisters on tops of my toes when I ran. But I loved them. I cleaned them and put new sharp spikes in them for every race. The long, 1/2-inch ones for cross-country season that would clack like mad when the field crossed the Macadam road.

That was another word I learned at age 11 or 12. Macadam, Mark called it. Never black top or road. Just Macadam. I had to look it up.

"Broken stone of even size used in successively compacted layers for surfacing roads and paths and typically bound with tar or bitumen." Named for 18th-19th century British surveyor John L. Macadam.

And that was why the Nike Elite—it was a rubber-soled racing flat. It had a waffle sole that today I find to be incredibly cool, but then, not so much.

The Eagle had a flat, smooth sole and we were running in grass and dirt and mud—and occasionally across or along the Macadam road so the

Elite was more perfect for the job than the Eagle. And it was more affordable.

I'd be older and faster when my dad agreed to get me something more—the Nike Triumph, my first pair of good spikes that didn't blister the tops of my toes like the old Adidas nameless nylon shoes. There was a pair of Adidas XC spikes with knobby soles toward the heels, too. We all wore them at one point or another.

Winter of my freshman year, my parents drove me into Manhattan to the Super Runner Shop. All the older guys had made the same journey the year before to get their Zooms. I remember watching them run in the beautiful, fast, spotless white shoes on the orange track surface inside the bowl of the stadium at the Rutgers Relays.

The blue swoosh with the plastic spike plate Carlotti ran in. The orange swoosh on the indoor model with the rubber covered spike plate designed for sticking to the dinged-up banked board tracks in places like Madison Square Garden and the Meadowlands. The sprint shoes with no heel I loved most. The shape of that thin sole cupping the heel looked so sleek with the dark blue swoosh one side and red on the other. Like running barefoot in Ancient Olympia.

The white shoes were always the fastest.

JJ Clark in his Red Columbia uniform on the black, hard track around Olcott Field in the 1980 Bernards Invite. Dark skin, red uniform, white shoes, looked so, so fast. Had to be fast. I wanted to be JJ with his cool name. I would get to know him later at Villanova and later still when I moved here to Colorado and we ran into him and his Stanford team on their summer altitude camp.

Steve Bailey loaned me his Nike Eagles to run the Springfield 10k one year when I was still in junior high. I'm still grateful.

Pete Carroll once gave me a pair of bright yellow Adistars that he got from Johnny Marsh. I ran in them at the state meet at Rutgers then in the state cross-country meet. We loaned and gave each other shoes all the time, but these were John Marshall's shoes. The great Villanova anchor man, Olympian, from Plainfield who ran 1:48 in high school.

The drive in and out of the city on little, local Route 24 because Route 78 wasn't completed yet. Madison. Chatham. Short Hills. Milburn. Track surface inside the store to try them out. I couldn't wait to race in them. Then the long ride home. They'd remain in the box until spring. Me just itching to lace them up. This was shoe buying in those days.

# 1982

# 27

"I can't seem to face up to the facts
I'm tense and nervous and I can't relax
I can't sleep 'cause my bed's on fire
Don't touch me, I'm a real live wire."

- Talking Heads

Cyclists say you save 30 percent of your energy drafting behind another rider. The math isn't exactly the same in running, but when you're in the midst of a pack of 20 or more sliding up Olcott Avenue toward Old Army Road in 90 degree heat starting a 10-mile trail run together, you feel like you're part of a machine much bigger than yourself. And, at least at the outset of your run, you're expending very little effort. Just breathing. Warming up. Shooting the breeze with your friends about what's really important in your teenage mind at that singular moment. Maybe you're paying attention to the shadows cast through the canopy of leaves. Maybe the way the gravelly surface of the crowned road feels through the soles of your Adidas Marathon Trainers. Maybe just how different everything smells today compared to yesterday.

There's spitting to the side and occasional snot-rockets, but nobody cares. Nobody judges. We just keep running. There are new shoes in the group, so there will be initiation at that low spot, the always muddy spot about halfway back to Flatrock.

We're still all together at the base of Old Army Road. We cross Hardscrabble together and hop from rock to rock crossing the stream to the Flatrock trail then start operating as a unit—single-file winding back and forth up and down under and over the fallen trees. There's a dip in the trail where everything widens out. It's soft and usually muddy in the middle and Mike Flood gives Stogryn a little shove to step his new trainers into the dark softness maiming the sparkling new shoes forever. There's yelling of objections and laughing and we keep going—out the straight trail to the clearing where the stream waterfalls into a shallow pool a couple of feet deep. A small swimming hole. We take a quick drink of the rushing stream water and head over, then up the switchbacks heading toward Jockey Hollow.

And this is where the group starts to string out. The pace quickens and things start to get a little serious. On the far side of the switchbacks, the trail narrows to just a hint of a bare dirt line through bright green ferns. The earth is soft and smooth until one tree root reaches up and grabs me by the laces and I start to topple head-first into the coffee grounds earth under foot. After I slide to a halt on my belly, I clamber up and strike out to catch up. Rory Farrell is laughing at me saying it took ten seconds for me to hit the ground—like slow motion "tiiiiimmmmbeerrr!"

The woods break where the course crosses Tempe Wick Road into the proper part of the National Park. This is where Washington's troops wintered in 1779-1780. A worse winter than the one that decimated the Continental Army at Valley Forge.

The trail opens up here to what would be a colonial carriage road between two colonial-era split-rail fences to the visitor center where we get another quick drink. This time from a water fountain opposite a full-scale diorama of a colonial officers cabin.

Then, it's back into single-file formation to the back side of the Scherman Sanctuary and up Old Army Road to home. Ten miles. Summer trail run. Mostly dry feet.

I loved running in the trails most of all. It was away from the road and cars. We moved as a group in line almost like a single living organism. Sometimes we were in small groups. We weren't supposed to run alone back there in case we turned an ankle, but sometimes we did.

I remember one time with rain clouds looming. There was a downpour hanging in the sky above the trees. There was that that feeling in the air. The hair on your arms going up. That weird smell in the air. Ozone. Rumbling in the sky over there. Over there. You couldn't really tell under the trees. Fifty, sixty, seventy-five, and a hundred year old oak trees all around.

I'm running up and away past Flatrock deeper into the woods and having that feeling like someone is chasing me. So I'm picking up the pace. Trying to get away from... nothing. And there's this sound. Loud. So loud. Crrraaaaack! Like a bang or a gunshot. I look back and there's a streak of fire spiraling down the trunk of one huge tree. It bounced me forward off the ground and threw me into the air.

I can hear the sound of the rain starting on the canopy of the woods. Harder and harder, but not wet yet. The leaves are too dense. It took a full three, five minutes it seemed for the water to start filtering down onto the dirt path. Then it was a drenching rainstorm. Like a downpour inside the green room.

And I'm running through the trees with nowhere to duck under for shelter. So I keep running. I pick up the pace and head up the hill and to the left. I know this goes back to Hardscrabble and Mt. Kenya and up and again behind some back yards to the back side of The Polo Grounds. By the time I crest the hill with the African name, the electricity of the storm has passed. It's still raining, but no more lightning I can feel coming.

I head back to the high school as quick as I can and inside my car. I have no idea of the time. I forgot to start the watch today.

# WORKOUT: 20 x 100m

My favorite. This is a workout that came later, much like the 20 x 400m version. But they both served different purposes. The biggest thing for me was doing a workout I LOVED that gave me confidence—a ridiculous amount of confidence without wearing me out too much. We started doing it during Carlotti's senior year so that gave us something to shoot for and measure against.

Like many of our workouts, we would put a time on the full duration of the workout and at the same time, individual splits for each fast piece. What we needed was the elapsed time of everything—all 20 fast pieces plus all the jogging beginning to end, AND we needed the cumulative time of all 20 100m repeats. All done in spikes after a warmup of a couple or three miles and stretching. Warm-down the same on the back end.

The most difficult thing was to start and stop the watch while sprinting. Usually, we'd take the watch off our wrists and hit the button with the thumb in one hand as we cruised across the line in a rolling start.

First: 100m fast. As fast as you could go. Starting at the start line and running the first turn first. Then slow to a quick trot for 200m then fly into the next 100m. After #20, we'd have to trot one full 400m to complete the circuit for 6400m total. Just short of 4 miles.

The record for the workout was 4:08. That's less than 12.5 for each 100m.

## THE WORKOUT: 20 X 100M

1 x 100m sprint

200m interval jogging.

x 20

+ 400m cantor around the oval to finish.

Now. Warm-down.

Seems simple. But in practice, not so much.

## SPIKE UP!

The watch accumulates all 20 100m intervals. It's a weird feeling to a distance runner at first. With little experience trying to maximize or optimize speed. We're just trying to turn over the legs as fast as possible. teaching our bodies to run faster than we do naturally. Hit the line fast—wrist watch in the palm of your right hand so it's easy to hit the start/stop and not reset. Lengthen the stride. Shorten it. Drive the knees high and hard. Feel the hip flexors pull and pull and pull. Remember what you learned from Choc in the stands in Philly. Feel the spikes pierce the track surface step after step—like a soft paddle on the recovery—tip tap tip tap. Across the stones of a creek, keeping the tempo staccato until the next corner of the oval. Then drive! drive! drive! It's only 100m at a time, after all. Coaching on form and biomechanics helps, but there's nothing quite like feeling where the speed comes from and leaks out. Shoulders and elbows. Knees and ankles. And the pitch of your upper body. Feel yourself leaning out over the tips of your spikes—almost falling face first onto the striped surface.

That was four—next starts at the start line again. Then 8. Then 12 down, 8 to go. Four miles in your spikes. Hands to your face. Snap them at the top of your shorts. Knee parallel to the ground. 14 done. Keep at it. Run the turn like Calvin Smith. Drive that right hand in, no flailing. Slide out as you cross the line at the end of the turn. Let the momentum carry you out to lane three. Lane four. You'll get back to the pole for the next one. Breathing hard but not as bad as some days—it's not that kind of workout.

16 done. Last 4 to go. Make them good. Hold the form you just spent the last 16 repeats finding. Don't let it fall apart here. Flying down the back stretch feeling the quads and calves working in warlike opposition. 19. One straightaway left. You've been picking up the pace on the interval over the past 8 or 10. Keeping one of many thoughts on the total accumulated time—that's important, too—you have a feeling. Sprint through the last finish line carrying speed into the turn. One short trot to the lonely 200m mark. Then one more 400m cantor to make it 6400m. Almost four miles for a cumulative time. Feeling the aching effort in your legs. The burn on the balls of your feet. The "just one more around" feeling between your ears.

4:08 for the fast 100m repeats. 2000m.

16:24 + 4:08 + :90 = 22:02 or about 5:34/mile.

This was the day. Mark was angry and frustrated about something. Watching us work out from the infield as usual. He shouted across to the home stretch where I was running between fast bits.

"Lyle! Are you doing these as fast as you're supposed to?"

"I'm doing them as fast as I can!" I called back. Reacting. Angry inside.

I saw a surprised look on his face standing there leaning on an umbrella stuck in the turf softened by the light rain. I didn't even raise my voice. And in the end, I ran the all-time record for that workout that day. We didn't really keep records for workouts. We just remembered them. And that was the only time I ever heard Mark raise his voice to anyone in anger or frustration.

# The running logs

I remember getting my first one. It was under the Christmas tree. It had that same picture on the cover. The striated calf muscle in the red Tiger racing flat from the Jim Fixx book.

It was the same book all the other guys had. Date. Day. Miles. Total. Room for the weather. How I felt that day. I wasn't as good at it as some of the guys. But I kept a log for years. And sometimes it helped to go back and look at what I'd done in the past.

I can't find any of them now. Maybe mom tossed them. Maybe they're in a box in storage? I hope that's where they are.

Jim Fixx, the author of "The Complete Book of Running," and one inspiration of the running boom who would later, ironically, expire from a heart attack. He may or may not have been running at the time.

The only one I have now is the one I used when I was coming back from my foot injury in 1988. It's helpful and painful to look at. Mainly because I know the end to that particular story. Or at least the end so far.

I wish I could go back and look at all that stuff now.

## Parents & Heroes

# 28

"A hero is an ordinary individual who finds the strength to persevere and endure in spite of overwhelming obstacles."

- Christopher Reeve

So much of this book is about growing up. Parents and families and heroes and what you know and what you don't know and figuring out your place in the world. My parents moved us to Bernardsville when I was about four in about 1972 when they were about 30, 31. Before that, we were living in my parents' hometown of Perth Amboy that dates back to before the revolution. They say there are tunnels from that time under the Raritan River that cross to the Billop House on Staten Island where they negotiated prisoner exchanges and cease fires. It was a working town. Mostly Irish and immigrant Poles, then later Slovak. Then later in the 50s and 60s, Puerto Rican and Dominican. My parents loved where they came from, but wanted a different environment for my sister and me to grow up. Better schools. More opportunity. And Bernardsville hit the nail on the head.

They bought #20 Stevens Street within walking distance of the train station. My dad rode the train back and forth into New York City for years to his career job at AT&T. He wasn't the only one in town to travel

travel this way every day. #20 was on top of a hill and walking distance to the Marion T. Bedwell school and The Polo Grounds, the high school, the Bernardsville Public Library, the movie house, the Woolworth, Sid Sussman's store. Pretty much everything was a walk or a bike ride away. As teens, we claimed boredom. As adults looking back on it, I couldn't imagine a better place to grow up.

When I came to running, a lot of the parents knew each other. My folks knew Chris Hallinan's mom. She came to my mom's famous New Year's Eve parties. The Beckwiths and the Meyers lived next door to each other. I remember Paul Stogryn's mom was active in the boosters for the Bernards Invitational and his step-dad drove a bunch to North Carolina for a meet. Twice. My dad knew Mr. Flood from AT&T and they lived right across from the high school on Olcott Ave. Mark lived just out of town on Mine Brook Road. Meg Waldron's dad was Mayor. Not figuratively, the actual Mayor. Larry Sullivan's clan grew up on Old Army Road just above the high school. And later, when Ranjan's family moved into town, they moved into #14 Stevens St. The house between us was the Kulick family. Bob was in Ranjan's and my class, but he went to Delbarton and ran a pretty quick 800m for himself there. We used to joke we had 3/4 of a great 4 x 8 team on the street. Bob died too young in Thailand, too.

But that's just a handful of the people connected to this story. There are so many others who lived in town and just out. Some a few miles further down Rt. 202 in Bedminster like the Praisners. Or in Peapack or Gladstone or any of the other towns along our runs within the sending district.

One of my favorite sayings is "be careful what you think you know about a person. Because you're probably wrong." And when you're in your teens and 20s, you are constantly sure you're right about everything.

My mom wanted more than anything to be a great writer. She was a great English teacher and drama teacher and director. Her students still tell me how much they loved her. They call her by her first name, Agnes. But she questioned her writing. Her storytelling. She never devoted the time to her writing that she did to her teaching so as a result... It was like the secret to Bernardsville running success. There was no secret. There was only doing the work.

Mark always called my dad, Lyle, or Lyle Sr. (which is what Heather always called him), and my mother Mrs. Smith. He never told me why. He didn't need to.

Hero is a funny word. It gets thrown around often under wrong meanings. In big ways and small. Websters calls a hero someone who is admired for courage, achievements, or noble qualities. In storytelling, the hero is the protagonist. In mythology, or in the classics, a hero is someone who is of superhuman qualities. Sometimes semi-divine and in Greek terms has a heroic flaw that will lead to the hero's eventual downfall.

Heroes come in all sizes and shapes. The Russian journalist and opposition leader Vladmir Kara-Murza was poisoned and almost killed by Russian Autocrat Vladmir Putin. Twice. Largely for his criticism and activity in getting the Magnitzky Act passed in the United States - a law designed to freeze the assets of human rights criminals in Russia. Instead of staying outside of his home country where he was (mostly) safe, he returned to Russia to continue his work. To continue his work.

Putin had him arrested and thrown in prison on a trumped-up charge and a 25-year sentence. The Biden Administration managed to get him released as a part of a large prisoner exchange in 2024. He continues to speak out against Putin and his government and given the chance, would likely return to the country he loves to keep at it no matter the threat to his own safety.

This is what a hero looks like in real life.

But there are other types of heroes, too. As an 11- or 12-year-old, the older runners around me were bigger than life. Winners you want to emulate in effort and success. If you're lucky, these heroes evolve into mentors for you. Whether they know it or not.

As an adult, your heroes are fewer and farther in between. You need to take time to think about who they are and why you think of them that way. They may not be Kara-Murza-style patriots putting their lives on the line every moment of every day. They may just be people who overcame something you never imagined at the time. Someone who succeeded in life despite things standing in the way you might never have known or understood.

I met Jeff Simpson when we were in the seventh grade. He came to the Bernardsville Half Marathon one year and we met before the three-mile fun run. He had to remind me of this recently. Mr. Mather saw him out running along a Hunterdon County road one day and stopped his car to shout out to him and invite him to come training with us. Imagine, an adult man stopping his car to chat up a 12- or 13-year-old boy out for a run in the countryside in today's world?

Eventually, Jeff joined the Mine Mountain Road Department and started training with us. He and Brad Hudson would run from his house to the Pepack-Gladstone Train Station and ride the few miles into Bernardsville every day. Then, they'd reverse the ride after practice and head for home on foot.

Jeff lived with his mother out there in Hunterdon County. We became fast friends and I eventually started visiting him there. We've been great friends ever since. Even after living in different parts of the country. Even after not seeing each other very often for years at a time.

I always liked Jeff's mom. I didn't see her often, but she was always nice to me. I never knew, nor understood why Jeff's brother lived with his father in White Plains. I guess because I was a kid, I never asked. I never wanted to be nosey. Now, years later, I understand his mom had problems of her own that cascaded over into daily life for Jeff. He attended Voorhees High School through cross-country season of freshman year, but then they moved into Bernardsville, where he really wanted to be. She did what she could to get him there.

Jeff committed himself to training with us. He grew into a truly great high school athlete and eventually running me into the ground on cross-country courses all around the state. I sometimes wish I dedicated myself more to the longer distance season the way he did and wonder how fast I could have gone if I did. But I decided I was really a track-man and couldn't figure out how to run that opening hill at Holmdel anyway, so...

## FEBRUARY 2024

I took Aiden to an indoor meet at CU. I wanted to introduce him to Mark and see what a big-deal college environment looked and felt like. He enjoyed the meet even though it was below zero outdoors.

When we found Mark, we were able to sit and chat for awhile and catch up. He asked Aiden questions and seemed to enjoy his company. I pointed out a few of Mark's former athletes who were there, leaning on the railing watching the meet along with us. Adam and Kara Goucher. Jorge Torres.

"Those two are olympians," I said. "And that guy there ran the World Cross-Country Championships."

Aiden was amazed. He asked Mark about how many Olympians he'd coached and Mark pointed to a few banners in the field house. I wanted to go over and introduce Aiden to some of these people, but I felt a little timid about it.

"You can talk to them," Mark said. "You've shared a lot."

Funny thing is Aiden is now teammates at Niwot High School with Addy Ritzenhein. National cross champ and daughter of Dathan Ritzenhein who ran for Mark and became a three-time Olympian himself. Brad Hudson coached him for a time, too. And he's not the only Olympian parent linked to the team. There are at least three parents on my son's cross-country team who are Olympians including Shayne and Alan Culpepper.

I remember when I was turning fourteen. I invited Jeff to celebrate my birthday with me. My parents took us out to dinner in Morristown. Cutters Grill, where I'd decided I had the best Italian food I'd ever had before. And being 14, I was an expert. It was just Jeff and me. Birthday parties weren't a thing in my house. But that was maybe the best, closest thing I could do with and for a friend in those days. I was grateful he came and I think he enjoyed himself.

I still don't know exactly how hard Jeff had it growing up. He lived in several different places in Bernardsville through his high school career. And I never asked why. I just decided the best thing I could do was be a good friend to him.

He had a great senior cross-country season. Ran great at the US World Team trials where he finished first high-schooler. Ran leadoff on our

Penn Championship of America Distance Medley. Managed to get an invitation to the International Prep Invitational (IPI) in Chicago at the end of the season to run a pretty darned good 3,000m steeplechase and land a partial scholarship to run for Doug Brown at the University of Tennessee.

The invitation came a week after the New Jersey State Meet of Champions. The International Prep Invitational in Chicago. Evanston, actually. Me in the mile run and Jeff for the steeple. So we all went back into tune-up mode with everyone else done for the season. On our travels, we crossed paths with Ron Faith from Paul VI and Kevin Pumphery from Highland Regional who were also invited to what was then known as Keebler.

It was an interesting experience, running post-season. We became chummy with our fellow NJ invitees and met numerous others. Trautmann was there, too. It was the first time I remember running for myself first rather than for the team. There was a hospitality suite in the hotel filled with Keebler products, which was great. The weather was roasting. And I ran what I felt was a memorably bad race. One I'd think about for... Ok, I still think about it. Then I jumped into the steeple pit up to my knees to cool off. I was not the only one.

So... heroes. People you want to be like at any given time in your life. They are your parents, your coaches, your teammates. Dad, Mom, Mark. The Chocolate Man. Grandparents. Larry Sullivan. The people who taught you things.

Jeff's story is a sort of wandering funny one. He stopped running competitively one day, left the Tennessee team and joined the circus. More precisely, a rock and roll band. A good one. The Clintons. He played lead guitar. They had an album. And tours. And fans. And eventually, he went and got his MBA at Tennessee. And a fantastic career. And he married Jennifer, who is as spectacular for him as Heather is for me. And they had their sons, Griffin and Lucas. And now he's a bit of a gentleman farmer. With a car collection. And he's good at all of it. And I sometimes still think of him driving us to the Meadowlands to see Van Halen for the second time in a week in his dark blue Volkswagen Scirocco.

And whenever I talk to him, he helps me figure things out.

And whenever I think about where he came from and the challenges he grew out of and beyond, I think... yes. Today, as an adult, he's a hero of mine.

I have no idea what he'd think about that. Or say to me. Or if he'd let me keep this in the book if I let him read it before I put it out. But that's what he is to me. And I think that's important to have. People you think of as heroic in your life. Even as an adult. Someone you can't ever be jealous of, but someone you can take inspiration from.

And he's not the only one I grew up with I think about in that way.

# WORKOUT: The Master Blaster: Part Deux

### DECEMBER 1985. MONDAY. OLCOTT FIELD.

Christmas break. Just as the year was turning 1986. We met in the basement hallway outside the upper gym where it was warm. Stretching. Kibbitzing. Goofing around together before we learned what the workout would be.

It was that wasted week between holidays. School was out but practice was in. Some years, we raced at Christmas City out at Lehigh. Some years, there was an open meet at Jadwin. This year, we were training.

Ranjan and I were sitting with Steve O'Hearn from Mendham who was training with us for the winter. A Morristown Beard School grad getting ready to transfer to UVa, Steve somehow got connected with Mark and he thought it would be a helpful push for us in training that winter.

"Hey Mark, what're doing today?"

"Some quarters."

This, by itself was worrying. We never did just a set of repeat quarters on the track like it was 1968.

"How many?"

"Oh... 16."

"Ha! That's a funny joke."

And we finished stretching and went out into the cold for a warm-up run.

When we came back into the warmth to pick up our spikes on the way out to the track. We asked again.

"Quarters? How many?

"Sixteen."

"Yeah, right, funny."

So the three of us, Ranjan the 800m guy, Steve, the graduate miler between schools, and me, we gathered up our gear, hit the head, then wandered out to the track to get a few strides in, spike up and strip down for our workout.

The rest of the team was out doing their own things when we got there.

"Spike up! Do some strides.," Mark said.

"So, how many quarters?"

"Sixteen," he said.

"Uh oh," we thought.

We stepped up toward the line and Mark gave us the breakdown.

"It's a little cold today (32 degrees) and breezy, so I'm going to give you a little reprieve," he said. "We were going to do 400s in 60 seconds (about 4-minute mile pace), but because of the weather, lets go 62s."

We stood there in tights and long sleeves. Gloves to start. Rolling our eyes.

This would be a Master Blaster. Each of us three would lead a 400 in 62, then a 400 interval as fast or slow as we liked. Then the second guy would do the same. Then the third. If you got dropped on the interval and couldn't catch up before the next fast 400 started, you were done.

And you never wanted to be done.

We hit 62 on the first one and quickly turned the screws down to 60.

The intervals were, maybe a bit slower than Mark wanted, but nobody got dropped.

And we kept getting faster.

And the rest of the team kept finishing their workouts and leaving.

By the time we got to the eighth or ninth, we were the only ones left on the track. By eleven or twelve, a small group came back out of curiosity to check in on us.

We were under 60 now, over and over.

I could feel my calves knotting up.

Tom Praisner called out "you're STILL out here?"

"Just a couple left to go," I called back at the gate by 300m.

The last four were hard.

Really hard.

And the muscles in my legs were getting shorter in my Zoom sprint spikes.

But I wasn't backing down.

None of us were.

The last two were, in my memory, something a little special. I crossed the line first, but we were all in on each other. Number 15 was :54 and change and I limped my way to the fence to stretch my calves. I rushed to catch the other two on the back stretch of the final interval as we joked about how many more we'd have to do to win.

Number 16, we stepped toward the line, rolling start, hit the button on the Casio and off we went. First turn quick. Backstretch accelerate. Far turn, where we'd usually just carry speed, we started challenging each other. 150 to go and we were shoulder-to-shoulder and one right behind accelerating onto the straight. Crossed the line in :52.5.

The three of us, together, started jogging the next interval together. We had to go another one.

"That's it. Good work." Mark called to us.

"But we need to do..."

"No. That's enough."

And I spent the next three days stretching my calf muscles back to their original length. I know there are teams and individuals who have done harder, longer workouts. Faster. But that was, bar-none, one of the most memorable afternoons of my life.

We slipped on our sweats and jogged a little bit to warm down. But my calf muscles wouldn't let me do much. There was a hot bath in my future. We lost touch with Steve not long after that season. And we've lost Ranjan. So I'm the only one with first hand memory of that workout. I'm sure Mark has a different memory of it. I kinda wish I could ask Ranjan what he remembers.

Who was the Master Blaster, in the end? All of us finished and kept in. If you totaled our precise aggregate times, they'd probably be within a second of each other. Then Mark threw up the flag. So I say there wasn't one.

# Never a Disappointment

# 29

"Silent gratitude isn't much use to anyone."
- Gertrude Stein.

The National Collegiate Athletic Association (NCAA), in it's infinite wisdom, decided in 1986, that the watches presented as trophies to the championship athletes at the Penn Relays would henceforth be considered "merchandise" and therefore against recruiting rules for the high school athletes to receive.

Penn, having absolutely no recourse, pulled the watches and awarded the members of their high school Championship of America teams... nothing.

If you are not familiar, the NCAA has a long history of poor, misguided, illogical, and often self-defeating decisions in very public ways.

The University of Pennsylvania began presenting gold watches to it's winning Penn Relays teams in 1925. For generations, the watches have been gold, Hamilton mens' and women's models with the letters P-E-N-N-S-Y-L-V-A-N-I-A replacing the numbers 1-12 on the face.

I received one for being a part of the Bernards 1984 team.

## FRIDAY, APRIL 24, 1986

We'd run the fastest high school time in the country for the Distance Medley Relay indoors back in December. The team ran 10:16 at West Point and I'd run the fastest anchor of my life in 4:12.5. It was the second-fastest indoor distance medley of all time after Bernards 1983 at the same venue. Despite the fast indoor times, we were always considered a bit of an underdog at Penn. We didn't mind, really. We knew what we were capable of.

We arrived in Philadelphia on Thursday to watch the girls run their 4 x 800m Championship heat and check into the Sheraton so we could be fully rested to run Friday afternoon. We'd run well in Virginia and felt confident, but standing in the paddock looking up at that very large crowd was enough to shake anyone's nerves.

Jeff took the stick to the line in his tall, black socks and hung with the middle of the pack through the first two laps and ran up the heels of the leaders on the last to hand off in a very close fourth. Greg Mallek grabbed the handle of the red and blue baton and held his own against some very fine sprinters to get the stick to Ranjan about twelve meters down.

I'd joked with Ranjan the night before jogging around the stadium track. I stood at the top of the exchange zone on the inside rail where I'd take the baton from him tomorrow with my hand out and said "this is where I want to be tomorrow afternoon."

He just said, "ok."

At 4:55:03 in the afternoon the next day, he did just that. Ranjan battled through the crowd on the first lap of his carry, hung patiently in second place through about 700m, then emphatically took the lead.

I took the stick from him and led out the field for the next four laps. With no watch in our future, I was absolutely, positively sure I was going to get the victory to take home, at least.

Simpson (3:07.9), Mallek (:51), Sinha (1:54.3), Smith (4:13.7) 10:06.9

I held onto the baton and made sure we went out for a victory lap. First one of the meet that year. If the blue blazers of the NCAA were going to deny us our watches, I wanted to be sure we got something for the effort.

Almost a year later. The NCAA changed its mind. No apology. No "kiss my..." Just a change of ruling. Penn, in an act of superior generosity, made sure all the high schoolers who did not get their watches a year before, received them before the meet in 1987.

I had mine engraved with the date of the race, the event H.S.D.M. for High School Distance Medley, and the time. I gift-wrapped the Hamilton box and brought it with me to Franklin Field on Friday of the Carnival weekend in 1987. I found Mark sitting in the stands along the back stretch with the Seton Hall team he'd been assistant-coaching that year. We chit-chatted for a few minutes, then I handed him the package saying something like, "I just wanted to say 'thank you.'"

He looked at me suspicious and opened the box. To say he was surprised would be an understatement. He was as I've never seen him before. Speechless. I already had a watch from 1984. I didn't really need two. You can only wear one at a time. But seriously, I felt he deserved it as much or more than any of us.

# Millrose

# 30

*"You may be disappointed if you fail, but you are doomed if you don't try."*

- Beverly Sills

We took a Rent-a-Wreck into the city for the 1986 Wanamaker Millrose Games and it was. The exhaust system is probably still lying along the side of the NJ Turnpike extension under the Pulaski Skyway somewhere. We finished the drive sounding like the Staten Island Ferry pulling into the terminal at Whitehall. I have no idea why we took that huge station wagon that night, but I'm sure there was a reason.

My folks and my grandparents and the rest of the spectators would be up in the stands looking down on the little 11-lap to the mile track. I'd be underneath everything with Mark and my teammate Karen Ahearn who was invited to run the girls race, and all the other coaches and athletes and officials where the Knicks and the Rangers and the Ringling Brother's Elephants usually hang out.

One of the most famous track & field events, ever, The Wanamaker Millrose Games moved to the Armory in Washington Heights in 2011. And while the track there and the facility are vastly superior for running fast, I have to say we lost something when the meet moved uptown away from The Garden.

Named after the Cheltenham, PA, country home of Department Store Magnate John Rodman Wanamaker, Millrose, the track meet, began in 1908 on the roof of the Philadelphia store and moved to Madison Square Garden in 1914 where it was contested every year in New York City from before the Great War through the Great Depression, survived all the other oddball sporting events like the six day bicycle races and endurance walking throughout the WWII years, the 50s, and the 60s to the economic anxieties of the 70s. It survived the 1980 Olympic boycott and was one of the things that enabled US athletes to compete at the highest level even without an Olympic dream realized.

Millrose was the most glamorous thing I'd ever seen in person when I first sat in the nosebleeds in 1979. The meet officials all dressed in tuxedos. Kurt Steiner running all over the wooden floor moving stars from start to finish to interview locations.

I saw Olympians and world record holders up close. Celebrities were out for the night like the Hollywood stars who fill the floor seats at Lakers games.

People still smoked in those days so there was a steady weather pattern of blue tobacco smoke wafting through the rafters. To this day, I don't know how the runners lived with it. A different time, I suppose.

The voice announcing results and all the excitement was infectious. Then the house lights dimmed and it was time to stand for the National Anthem sung by Olympic gold medalist Madeline Manning Mimms. As the applause died down, the voice of the announcer came through in an unmistakeable echo. "Ladies and gentlemen. The Wanamaker Mile!" The signature event. The whole meet experience was so shiny. I so wanted to a part of it.

When I finally got there to run, I never felt so overwhelmed in my whole life. I should have just looked around the shabby warehouse space under the stands where they put us to warm up before the meet and adjusted my thinking. No great shakes. But that's not the way I was built. This was Millrose. One word. My mind was on the tuxes and lights and cameras and the glistening speed out on that wooden stage.

And make no mistake, that was what it was. A stage with an audience of 17,000 people in person and I don't know how many in TV-land. I'd run in front of more at Penn, but this was right on top of you. Cameras in your face. The building shook with applause and cheering and energy like nothing else.

I walked the length and breadth of the building several times. Checked in and got my race number. Spotted some of my heroes. Leaned on the bank of the track and watched Dwight Stones and Frank Shorter interview people on the infield.

I walked and jogged and stretched—closed my eyes and listened to music on my Walkman hoping I brought extra batteries. But mainly, I was worried. Expending energy with every movement. With every nervous heartbeat. I shouldn't have. It was just a race, after all. Like so many before.

I saw Steve Scott and Sydnee Maree—Marcus O'Sullivan and Eamonn Coughlin. Miler-Gods. Some of whom I'd meet and even get to know later. But in the moment, it was like seeing Mount Rushmore standing up and jogging around the same place you were allowed to be.

We weren't scheduled until just before the Wanamaker Mile. At 9:45 pm. A time none of us was used to for racing. Most of my life to that point I went to bed by 10:00 p.m.

The girls mile was up earlier in the night. Scheduled for 8:40 p.m., Karen raced against the best in the country like Shola Lynch and Jasmin

Jones and Erin Keough. I'm sorry to say I didn't see her race. I heard she fell in the early laps. A pole-vaulter kicked the crossbar on his way up and the bar came down hard on the track at Karen's feet. She tripped and fell and slid down the bright colored stripes of the track bank. True to her nature, she got up and raced her way back into contention. I'm sure she was disappointed. I remember there being tears. The TV announcer said third, but I'm not sure.

"No way did I come here to finish last!" she told me later.

I was all up in my head. Didn't want to let things distract me. That may have been a mistake. Probably was.

I remember stepping out onto the track thinking I was wearing the wrong spikes. I picked the Zoom sprints instead of the orange swoosh indoor shoes. It probably didn't matter. There were bigger things to think about. Bigger decisions to make. Bigger mistakes.

I looked up at the crowd—some 17,000 strong—and saw my grandfather calling out to me. His little head soooooo far up—smiling at me.

They held us on the line for what seemed like forever. There was a guy with a TV camera on his shoulder in my face. I was second from the outside. Waaaay out on the California stagger. I just wanted to get racing. John Trautmann was back on the main start line. I kept shaking out my legs over and over and over again. Twitchy. Nervous. Very nervous.

Then... Runners set! And we stepped to the line to listen for the gun.

I almost fell off the top of the bank on the first turn. Then, I felt like the only way to get—stay out of danger on the tight turns—was to slide up on the outside. The track felt like running in a teacup. The steep downhill of the bank from the outside carried me to the front. And there I was. Out of trouble, yes, but not where I wanted to be. A sitting duck.

I slowed down to let someone pass. Anyone. But no one came. I was all alone at the front of a very slow race with a bunch of very fast guys behind me. Guys I didn't really know. So I just led for the time-being. And everybody else seemed perfectly satisfied with that. Until two laps to go. Less than a quarter. Johnny Trautmann took the lead with Kevin Robinson from Vancouver right behind.

All of a sudden, I had nothing left in the tank. Both Mastelir brothers went by waving from California. And Norm McHugh from Connecticut. I couldn't react. I tried. But I was cooked. Just a spectator now. It felt like I was running in pudding. And the race was over. That was my Millrose Experience.

Disappointment didn't come close to describing what I felt. Every wrong decision. I always thought of myself as a pretty savvy racer. Now I felt wrong. Demoralized.

We hung out to watch the rest of the meet. I watched Marcus O'Sullivan beat Eamonn Coughlan and the rest to stake out his claim on the Wanamaker Trophy.

Walking around in a fog, Mark pulled me aside. He told me he knew I was disappointed but he was proud of the way I ran. He knew it was slow and nobody wanted it, so running from the front was the only way. It was courageous, he said. And that made me feel a little bit better.

I've had that experience with Mark a few times. When he seemed to know things no one else did. Things no one else could possibly understand. So often the insight was uncanny. And always at the right time.

Like when I let Dan Gough of Haddonfield just run away from me in the State Group I 3,200m at Jadwin. He asked me if that was the best I had. It wasn't. Then he told me to go sit by myself and get my head together for the 1,600m. I sat at the top of the stands—lying on my back. When the time came, I walked back down to the track and trounced everyone in the field.

At the Colonial Relays when I'd been miserably depressed and distracted in teenage angsty love—Welcome to Dumpsville. Population: you.—he told me he was proud of the way I'd conducted myself after anchoring the 4 x 800m to our second win of the weekend.

There was Keebler. The International Prep Invitational in Chicago. What a nervous train wreck. Almost the same field as Millrose. It was so hot, I was not the only one to jump into the steeple pit to cool off. I was dejected, and embarrassed, and broken down by what had just happened. Mark was kind. He was always kind. Always looking to what's next.

I think that is the one thing people don't understand about Mark Wetmore, he pays more attention than anyone I've ever known. More attention to the people in his charge. And he cares deeply. People think of him as this oddly magical character. Sometimes Merlin. Sometimes Svengali. But he's really just a guy who cares deeply about what he's working to achieve and the people he's working with. And that, I think, is the secret to his success. He's proud of accomplishments, sure, but he's always looking forward and that's what I have to keep reminding myself of. And what I try to teach my son. It's hard. It's supposed to be hard. And that's ok. It's what makes it great.

A few minutes after the embarrassment of my Millrose collapse, I was walking around at the top of one of the banked turns watching the

races and I was approached by this other athlete. I recognized her face, but couldn't name her. I couldn't understand her hardly at all in her deep accent. Eastern European. Russian? No. Romanian.

Through gestures and a few shared syllables, I began to realize she really liked the tights I was wearing.

They were awesome to be sure. Red and blue horizontal stripes that changed thickness up and down like a wave and made them sometimes look purple. She was offering me a brand new pair of Adidas tights still in the package to swap. Sure! Why not? New's better than old, I thought. Stripes are better than Eastern Bloc, she was thinking. And I stripped my tights right there and swapped with Doine Melinte of Romania. Olympic gold medalist. World Champion. Who'd just won the women's 1,000m thirty minutes before my race.

Fun. And weird. And memorable. I hope she enjoyed the tights.

fin

# 31

"One can be a brother only in something.
Where there is no tie that binds, men are not united,
but merely lined up."

- Antoine de Saint-Exupery, French poet and aviator

My grandfather was standing alone in the kitchen when the phone on the wall rang. He picked up the receiver and answered in the same friendly "hello," he always did.

"Ernest Smith?" the voice said.

"This is he," he said.

There was a pause on the other end. And the static of a long distance call.

"Ernest Lyle Smith?" asked the voice.

"Yes. That's me."

There was another pause on the line. As if there was some confusion.

"The Ernest Lyle Smith who visited the University of Texas Hospital in Houston in 1975?"

"Yes. That's me."

"Please hold for Dr. Cooley," the voice said.

A few moments later, the receiver on the other end of the line clicked in.

"I thought sure you'd be dead by now!" said the semi-familiar voice of Denton Cooley. My grandfather laughed out loud.

My grandfather had severe heart disease and his first heart attack by the time he was 45 years old. He was a smoker since he was a kid in tiny Owego, New York. He survived several cardiologists who told him he wouldn't live out the week. And in 1975, he traveled to Houston, Texas to see Dr. Denton Cooley, arguably the greatest cardiac surgeon ever who famously implanted the first-ever fully artificial heart. The open-heart surgery he did on my grandfather was basically a repair job. He sewed in a silk patch over where a large weakening of the heart muscle was. Basically a patch on an aneurism.

This phone call was 1990. Fifteen years after the night Cooley came to see him in his hospital room. They were doing follow-up on results with patients in their files. Cooley may have been writing about it.

The night before the truly frightening procedure, the surgeon visited him in his room and asked how he felt and if he had any questions. My grandfather, forever curious, asked, "So, I understand this is an experimental procedure."

"Yes," said Cooley.

"How many other guys have you done this surgery on?"

"Two."

"And what happened to them?"

[Long pause]

"They both died on the table."

My grandfather paused and thought for a moment.

"So if I don't have this surgery, how long do you think I have?"

"You might live to the end of the week."

[Long pause]

"Ok," he said. "You should get some rest. You've got to work in the morning."

Cooley laughed, shook my grandfather's hand, and left the room. And after my grandfather woke up the next day after the successful procedure, Denton Cooley never did that surgery again. Ever. It was deemed "too dangerous."

My grandfather's health had improved enough to go on regular walks and even play golf with me from time to time. He walked about five miles every morning very early and, among other things, picked up the morning papers at the local news stand in Perth Amboy down near the waterfront. For years. All through my high school years

It's a small world, newspapers. And in New Jersey, like everywhere else, the truckers and pressmen and composing room workers are all union. And they all know each other. And they all like to talk. And they like the good stories more than the controversial stories they have to print every day.

I always wondered why The Home News, the paper of record in Middlesex County started covering us, big featured photos in the sports section after our big meets. We couldn't even get that paper in Bernardsville. But in my junior year, they did.

My grandfather knew the guy who ran the news stand. And he talked to the guys who drove the delivery trucks. And word got back somehow to the sports department that I was born in Perth Amboy which was in their coverage area. So they adopted me. And Bernards. And we got some awesome pictures as a result.

It's sometimes a very strange thing to come from a small town.

Track and cross-country are very different sports now than when I ran as a kid. All the teams are much more connected than they used to be. Friendlier. And I guess that's a good thing. We always had imaginary grudges against the rival teams in my day. Pfft. CBA!

But the way they run has changed, too. They're much more concerned with running fast than they are racing and winning, it seems to me. Running fast versus racing. It is a different mindset. They want to win, of course, but the strategic races don't set up the way they used to.

And with the Internet, they're able to track each other and see each other's workouts all the time. There's almost no excuse for having a bad coach anymore. Or bad information. And they don't put in the same miles we used to. Not to mention the facilities. We had some great surfaces to run on, but we also ran on gym floors sometimes, too. Even the cross-country courses are better maintained. Holmdel was all deep grass and tree-roots when I ran there. Today, there's a manicured path just about all the way 'round. Not to mention the super shoes and GPS watches and every other crazy technological development. I joke to Aiden all he needs is a Casio and a pencil.

Don't get me wrong, even with all of this stuff, these young athletes are ALSO running really, really fast. And that's a little amazing to see.

In the end, it's still a sport that's all about the joy. Watch any meet on any Saturday anywhere in the country and you'll see it. Especially in cross-country season. You'll see the top athletes who won the varsity race out cheering the last runners in the open race just to try and help get 'em home. And they'll all hang out and socialize and rehash their pain after the meet is done. Because the last-place runner hurts just as bad as the first-place runner and they all understand that. It's sometimes about the score and the time, but it's always about the effort.

You still have to go when the gun goes off and get to the finish line before everybody else. And there's this family of people I've known since I was small who are always happy to connect and talk and share old stories. And not just the racing stories. Or the championships. The stories about people and training and testing ourselves out there in the dirt and mud of Flatrock. About sliding down Ballantine Road in the snowy tire tracks behind the school bus. And outrunning the rain and lightning. And running up and down the stairs and hallways of the old Olcott Building when it was raining too hard to go outside. And remembering those tough races that didn't work out the way you had in mind. That time we ran the Somerset County meet on a muddy course on Halloween and I slipped and banged my forehead on a loose post on the inside of a turn. Finishing third with blood streaming down my face. They all thought it was a Halloween gag. It wasn't. And when you run into the people you once knew and pick up the conversation as if you'd spoken just yesterday. Or when you reconnect with Andy Martin who you knew better as a child or Ron Faith who you never really knew that well to begin with but shared a couple of great travel experiences and you talk for hours as if you were brothers. And you remember the people who are gone at any given moment of the day just because you're both connected to that incredible experience. Mather and Larry Sullivan and Ranjan. It's what it feels like to be sad and elated at the same time.

I was 100 percent sure of some things once. Then I was sure I was 100 percent wrong. I never ran with the Buffaloes. But I feel like I know them all. Even the ones I haven't met. Because I know a lot of the running the Buffaloes did came from the running we did on the Bernardsville Mountain. And all of that running came from the running Lydiard did with his athletes. Olympians to recreational health enthusiasts. And all of that running—all the blood, sweat & spikes—had a profound impact on the health and happiness of the world. And all of that running knowledge was shared and traveled all around the globe to far-flung places like the Rift Valley, and La Loma, and Puerto La Cruz, and Turku, and Myrskyla, and Helsinki, and Eugene, and Big Bear Lake and Boulder. And little Bernardsville in the Somerset Hills.

# Post Script

After I finished the writing of this manuscript, I sent it over to my coach and friend, Mark Wetmore. I wanted to give him a chance to see it before I started pushing it forward in any way. He gave me a couple of small details I didn't know about that beautifully filled in a few gaps. And for that I'm grateful. But he also told me something else that touched me deeply.

"I do not keep momentos. I have none of the trophies, rings, watches, Coach of the Year awards… I have felt that too easily anchors one to the past, and distracts from the potential of the future," he wrote to me.

"But I have your Penn Relays watch."

No, Mark. That's your watch.

# Acknowledgements

I have my son, Aiden, to thank, or maybe to blame, for this book existing in the world of real paper and ink at all. He gave me a notebook for Christmas. Then he committed himself to a summer of training for the Niwot High School cross-country team and me to a summer of dropping him off to practice at 7:00 a.m. every morning. This left me with an hour and a half or more on a stool in the open front window of The Old Oak Coffee House before picking him up after his run every day. I started scribbling longhand in that notebook with a vague idea of remembering. By the time the school year began, the contents of the small book was aching to be typed out to see what it wanted to be. This book is that thing.

There are so many people to thank behind this story becoming real, and concrete, and shareable. To Heather for being encouraging on one hand and never letting me off the hook on the other. Always forcing me to clarify. I mean it with intense love and gratitude when I say she challenges me and makes me better in every way possible every day. She is my perfect editor.

I have to thank several people for granting permission for me to raid their photo collections and the memories that go along with them. Thank you John Peterson (JP), Sharon Ahearn Siedleski, Jim Nielsen, Dr. Jennifer Rahn, and Holly Ahearn snapping and keeping these shots over the years. All other photos are from my father, Lyle Smith Sr.'s collection.

So many of the other people I'd want to acknowledge are already mentioned inside these covers. The parents and coaches and friends and mentors and competitors. They taught me things I remember and continue to try and put to use today. Sometimes things I didn't want to learn. Sometimes things I may some day forgive, but will never forget. They befriended me when I needed friends. Encouraged me when I needed encouragement. Inspired me when I needed inspiring. Knocked me down when I needed knocking. And helped me in every which way possible.

There are several friends who were generous with their time and energy in reading the early draft. Jill and Jerry Wichtel. Sung Woo. Dawn White. Rocket. Alex and Dave from Talking in Ovals. Thank you for your insight, Emily. It means more than you know. To Gary Gordon for caring and calling me back. To every track and cross-country fan out there for helping this amazing sport survive and thrive. To Steve Patrick for lending me his memory and encouragement and a couple of great quotes. To John Peterson for telling me to "suck up the embarrassment" and share the personal stuff. To Jeff Simpson for all that and more. To JJ Hagen, OSA, for not blinking when I told him I was choosing English as a major. To my dad and grandpop for telling me their stories. To Ed Grant for writing not just about me, but every kid in New Jersey who ever had a dream of running something important and telling the world that New Jersey Track mattered. To Ed Mather for every bit of his commitment to the sport and every bit of the confrontational, complicated relationship I had with him, see the "forgive and forget" reference above. To my home town of Bernardsville who whenever I return, however many years have passed, is so completely changed and yet so perfectly, exactly, predictably the same. And to Charles Mark Wetmore for helping us accomplish the things that were never done before and creating something meaningful to carry along with us forever.

## About the Author

Lyle Smith lives in the Boulder Valley drawing daily inspiration from his wife, Heather, a leading acupuncturist and fertility specialist in her field and his son, Aiden, a truly old soul who forever forces new angles from which to admire the world. Lyle's been a reporter, a caddie, a grave-digger, a marketing professional, and a runner since he discovered the sport as a youngster growing up in Bernardsville, New Jersey. You might see him out there running the trails around Boulder with his Golden Retriever, Elsa.

# Books & Other Works Mentioned in this Volume

The Power Broker: Robert Moses and the Fall of New York
Robert A. Caro | 1974, Vintage

Will in the World: How Shakespeare Became Shakespeare
Stephen Greenblatt | 2004, W. W. Norton

Running with the Buffaloes
Chris Lear | 2000, Lyons Press

Running the Lydiard Way
Arthur Lydiard & Garth Gilmour | 1978, World Publishing

That Championship Season
Jason Miller | 1973 Pulitzer Prize for Drama,
1982 film adaptation written & directed by Jason Miller

The Electric Cool Aid Acid Test
Tom Wolf | 1968, Farrar Straus Giroux

"The Wetmore Formula"
Jonathan Gault, with additional reporting by Mitch Kastoff | 2014, LetsRun.com

www.ingramcontent.com/pod-product-compliance
Lightning Source LLC
Chambersburg PA
CBHW071403130526
44581CB00015B/136/J